Blackstone

THE DATA GUIDEBOOK FOR TEACHERS AND LEADERS

D1450665

Special thanks to the following people for
their friendship, encouragement, and support:

Jeffrey Depka
Kay Burke
Heidi Laabs
The dedicated staff of the School District of Waukesha
Mom

THE DATA GUIDEBOOK FOR TEACHERS AND LEADERS

TOOLS FOR CONTINUOUS IMPROVEMENT

EILEEN DEPKA

CORWIN PRESS
A SAGE Publications Company
Thousand Oaks, California

Copyright © 2006 by Corwin Press.

All rights reserved. When forms and sample documents are included, their use is authorized only by educators, local school sites, and/or noncommercial or nonprofit entities who have purchased the book. Except for that usage, no part of this book may be reproduced or utilized in any form or by any means, electronic or mechanical, including photocopying, recording, or by any information storage and retrieval system, without permission in writing from the publisher.

For information:

 Corwin Press
A Sage Publications Company
2455 Teller Road
Thousand Oaks, California 91320
www.corwinpress.com

Sage Publications Ltd.
1 Oliver's Yard
55 City Road
London EC1Y 1SP
United Kingdom

Sage Publications India Pvt. Ltd.
B-42, Panchsheel Enclave
Post Box 4109
New Delhi 110 017 India

Printed in the United States of America

Library of Congress Cataloging-in-Publication Data

Depka, Eileen.
The data guidebook for teachers and leaders: Tools for continuous improvement / Eileen Depka.
    p. cm.
Includes bibliographical references and index.
ISBN 1-4129-1754-9 (cloth) — ISBN 1-4129-1755-7 (pbk.)
    1. Education—Research—Data processing. 2. Education—Research—Methodology. 3. Decision making—Data processing. 4. School improvement programs. I. Title.
LB1028.D442 2006
371.200285—dc22

                                                                2005031687

This book is printed on acid-free paper.

06 07 08 09 10 10 9 8 7 6 5 4 3 2 1

Acquisitions Editor:	Jean Ward
Editorial Assistant:	Jordan Barbakow
Production Editor:	Melanie Birdsall
Typesetter:	C&M Digitals (P) Ltd.
Copyeditor:	Cheryl Duksta
Proofreader:	Taryn Bigelow
Indexer:	David Luljak
Cover Designer:	Rose Storey
Production Artist:	Lisa Miller

Contents

List of Figures

Preface

The intent of *The Data Guidebook for Teachers and Leaders: Tools for Continuous Improvement* is to accentuate the importance of data collection and analysis within any educational setting. The data guidebook connects data collection to a continuous improvement cycle. This process identifies the purpose for data collection and analysis and places it into a system to improve student achievement.

This book outlines data collection and analysis. Tips on which data to collect, the identification of essential data, and the creation of a data balance are highlighted. The "data delve," a gathering of individuals to analyze data, is explained in detail, and organizational and reflective tools are included to assist in this process. Text regarding the organization of the delve provides step-by-step directions for planning and implementing a successful data experience. Techniques for building an atmosphere of trust and openness are included.

Information about collecting, reporting, and analyzing a variety of assessments is also included. Standardized tests, district assessments, and classroom evaluations are highlighted. Detailed information regarding a variety of reporting techniques is provided, along with references to tools to help others make sense of the data. Holistic and analytical rubrics are described, and examples of valuable rubric data are covered. A variety of classroom data uses are also discussed.

Throughout the book, there is an emphasis on working together while maintaining a focus on improved student achievement. Involving all of the key stakeholders in a data analysis and improvement process is recommended. Data analysis and reflection go hand in hand. There are examples of a variety of analysis and reflective activities that will aid in the process.

The book is full of examples and tools to enhance the use of data within classrooms, schools, and school districts. Data is promoted as an essential decision-making tool—data is knowledge. Analysis is not the end of the process but the beginning of a continuous improvement cycle.

This book is intended for use by individuals and groups who work within an educational setting, who have a connection to schools and districts, or who would like to know more about data and its connection to continuous school improvement.

ACKNOWLEDGMENTS

Corwin Press wishes to acknowledge the following reviewers for their contributions:

Joannie Kalina
Director of Curriculum
Kewaskum Elementary School
1415 Bilgo Lane
Kewaskum, WI 53040

Sharon Sweet
Administrator of Instructional
    Services
LAUSD District #6
5800 S. Eastern Avenue
5th Floor
Commerce, CA 90040

Jane Gaver
Curriculum Specialist
Davidson Elementary School
3915 E. Ft. Lowell Road
Tucson, AZ 85712

Deborah Beldock
Executive Director
San Diego City Schools
Eugene Brucker Education Center
4100 Normal Street
Room 2116 Educational Center
San Diego CA, 92103

Christelle Estrada
Director
Utah Staff Development Council
Professional Development
    Services
Salt Lake City District
440 East 100 South
Salt Lake City, UT 84111

Marlene Felix
Administrator of Instructional
    Services
LAUSD Local District #3
3000 South Robertson Blvd.
Suite 100
Los Angeles, CA 90034

Linda Thalacker
Educational Consultant: Standards,
    Assessment, and Data
6320 Charles Street
Racine, WI 53402

Rita J. Corbett
Teacher and Corwin Author
683 Bent Ridge Lane
Elgin, IL 60120

About the Author

 **Eileen Depka** is a veteran educator and currently works as the supervisor of standards and assessment for the Waukesha School District in Wisconsin. While focusing on assessment, she works with teachers and administrators to organize and use data as part of the decision-making and goal-setting processes in an effort to increase student achievement. With the No Child Left Behind legislation as a constant focus, she helps administrators and teachers share data and implement practices to meet improvement goals.

A regular presenter at both local and national conferences, she is the author of *Designing Rubrics for Mathematics* and the *Applying Mathematical Concepts* manual, as well as articles on mathematics, assessment, and data analysis. Eileen has served as a content adviser for educational videos, a writer of online courses, and an instructor of graduate-level courses in education.

Driving all of her work is her passionate belief that all students can achieve high levels of proficiency and her dedication to educators in their quest to help all students experience academic success.

1

Data-Based Decision Making and the Improvement Process

WHAT DO THE EXPERTS SAY?

It's all about continuous school improvement. Everything centers on student achievement. Article after article provide tips about improving student performance. Book after book include a variety of strategies outlined to increase student understanding. Excellent resources are plentiful. Without a focus, the use of these resources may have no impact on achievement. So what role do data play in the improvement process? Data supply the focus and identify the target. Through the collection and analysis of data, needs are recognized. Data-based goals are created. When incorporated into an improvement plan, impact on achievement is not only possible but likely.

According to Jones and Mulvenon (2003), an increasing amount of evidence supports the impact data have on student achievement. Jones and Mulvenon state that "when teachers and principals track student achievement systematically, they can make adjustments in the educational system that result in real improvements in student achievement" (p. 13).

When data are an integral part of the teaching, learning, and decision-making processes, a data culture can be established. All district stakeholders need to share the belief that data are an essential component of instructional decision making for students. "Good data are as much a resource as staff, books, and computers" (National Forum on Education Statistics, 2004, p. 3).

Data-driven districts provide the opportunity for administrators and teachers to work together in providing a district focus on student achievement. Everyone, including the superintendent, strives to achieve common data-based goals. "Data provide quantifiable proof taking the emotion" out of tough, but necessary, data-based decisions. (American Association of School Administrators, 2002, p. 1). The district becomes data focused and results oriented.

When reviewing a group of high-performing districts, the Educational Research Service found that these districts use multiple sources of data to guide decision making. Decisions are "based on data, not instinct" (Cawelti, 2004, p. 21). A well-balanced supply of data reviewed regularly will provide the basis for valuable observations and point toward potential solutions.

Time is an important component in the data review process. For data to have an effect on the improvement process, discussions need to occur. Rich conversations need to surround data collection and analysis. Data are turned into information; information is used to establish and pursue shared goals (Kline, Kuklis, & Zmuda, 2004, p. 87).

Although data analysis and the implementation of change can be seen as an arduous process, the resulting evidence of improved student achievement is stimulating. Success breeds success. Teachers become committed to the continuous improvement process (Danna, 2004, pp. 26–27).

Data review leads to the development of meaningful goals. In many cases, districts have similar, often impressive goals. When not data based, however, the goal may not be linked to student achievement or to an actual need within the district. The "emphasis on the data guards against seemingly impressive, but actually quite imprecise goals" (Schmoker, 2001, p. 36).

It is clear that the use of data needs to be an integral part of the continuous improvement process.

THE PROCESS

For data analysis to ultimately have an impact on student achievement, it needs to be part of a cyclical process. When data analysis is viewed as one step in a system, its use will become integral to the workings of the organization. Without a process, data analysis can be only an event. Time is spent viewing and analyzing data, but there is no intended result other than to comment on what is observed. Although time is not wasted, data viewed without a process will not likely become a catalyst for change.

THE IMPROVEMENT CYCLE

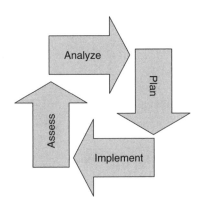

The following four-step process uses data as an integral part of an improvement cycle.

Step 1

Data analysis is a foundational part of the improvement cycle. Data provide evidence of system successes and challenges. The intent of analysis is to gather results that illustrate the effectiveness of current methods, procedures, and structures.

The Five W's (who, what, when, where, why) provide a summary of analysis components. More specific information is included in the chapters that follow.

Who should be involved in the analysis process? For data to become integral to the workings of the district, data must be shared and analyzed by all key stakeholders. Although the level and type of data may differ, opportunities for review should be provided for groups including, but not limited to, administrators, teachers, students, and parents.

What data should be analyzed? A combination of data needs to be collected and available to create a balanced picture of the school or district. Data should be viewed at the classroom, school, and district levels and include a balance of classroom, grade level, district, and standardized assessments. Attitudinal data can also be valuable to the process. Demographic and other nonassessment data help create a well-rounded view.

When should data be analyzed? Data reviews should take place as new data arrive. This may be weekly, monthly, or at select times of the year. Collective data should be reviewed annually. As questions arise, data should be reviewed as appropriate to assist in arriving at answers. Data should also be reviewed during program evaluation periods.

Where should data be collected? Data should be collected at places where it will be most effectively used. In other words, the classroom teacher collects a variety of data to make daily instructional decisions. School and district data, which would include performance, demographic, and attitudinal data, are important to collect at those levels. The data review group should consist of members who are affected by the results.

Why should data be analyzed? Data should be reviewed to evaluate all aspects of the classroom, school, and district as they relate to student achievement.

Step 2

The purpose of the analysis process is to review data to generate questions, ideas, conclusions, and comparisons, which, collectively, aid in the creation of an improvement plan. The intent of the plan is to answer the following question: What will we do about the results that we see? Improvement planning is not about what people want to do, or what they think they might want to focus on, but what the data tell them they need to do to increase the achievement of the students. Long- and short-term improvement goals are established.

Generating plans to reach goals requires the involvement of teachers and administrators at the school and district levels. At each level, plans need to be created that reflect the data. Classroom, school, and district plans should be mutually supportive. The district plan is developed to reflect challenges represented in the data at the district level. Through the analysis of school and district data, a school plan is developed. District results consist of collective school data; therefore, the plans will be mutually supportive. Classroom plans are designed to reflect classroom data as well as support school and district goals. Figure 1.1 illustrates one model that can be used for plan development. It highlights the components that should be considered before implementation. Figure 1.2 is the same planning form containing explanations and directions to better understand form components. The planning form can be typed into a table so that the sections can expand to meet the needs of the group.

Step 3

Plan implementation requires the involvement of all parties who are reflected in and affected by the plan. District staff should be knowledgeable and supportive. School staff should be clear on their key roles in the plan and its implementation. The involvement and support of students and parents is essential for the greatest impact on achievement. Analysis, planning, implementation, and assessment, although parts of a constant and continuous cycle, will likely be part of a three- to five-year plan.

Step 4

Assessment takes a variety of forms and is ongoing. Types and times of assessments are identified during the planning process. The goal is to assess the effectiveness of the plan throughout implementation. These assessment tools create a focus to evaluate the key components of the plan.

Figure 1.1   Improvement Planning Form

IMPROVEMENT PLANNING FORM		
District/School		
Identified Need From Data		
District/School Goals		
Improvement Plan Description		
Specific Improvement Plan Steps/Activities	**Person(s) Responsible**	**Time Frame**
Research to Support Improvement Plan		
Description		**Source(s)**
Assessment Plan		
Budget		
Item		**Cost**
Total		

Copyright © 2006 by Corwin Press. All rights reserved. Reprinted from *The Data Guidebook for Teachers and Leaders: Tools for Continuous Improvement,* by Eileen Depka. Thousand Oaks, CA: Corwin Press, www.corwinpress.com. Reproduction authorized only for the local school site or nonprofit organization that has purchased this book.

Figure 1.2   Improvement Planning Form Example

IMPROVEMENT PLANNING FORM
District/School
A planning form should be completed at the district level reflecting district information. It should also be completed for each school in the district reflecting their data and plans.
Identified Need From Data
Create a summary. What did the data reveal? What challenge areas surfaced? Be specific.
District/School Goals
As a result of the data analysis, what goals are indicated? The number of goals should be limited so that focus can be maintained. Goals should be specific and set within an achievement time frame.
Improvement Plan Description
How will the goals be achieved? What plans, programs, strategies, professional development opportunities, and so on need to be implemented to achieve the goals?

Specific Improvement Plan Steps/Activities	Person(s) Responsible	Time Frame
Provide information about the specific steps of the plan, including who is responsible for each step and when the step will be accomplished.		
Research to Support Improvement Plan		

Description	Source(s)
Plans need to be based on strategies that are believed to be successful. What research supports the ideas and steps outlined in the plan?	

Assessment Plan
How will the plan be evaluated? How will data be gathered and shared? What will be the indication of success?

Budget	
Item	**Cost**
Does the plan have a budgetary impact? What is needed and at what cost?	
Total	

Copyright © 2006 by Corwin Press. All rights reserved. Reprinted from *The Data Guidebook for Teachers and Leaders: Tools for Continuous Improvement*, by Eileen Depka. Thousand Oaks, CA: Corwin Press, www.corwin press.com. Reproduction authorized only for the local school site or nonprofit organization that has purchased this book.

Figure 1.3   The Complete Improvement Cycle Diagram

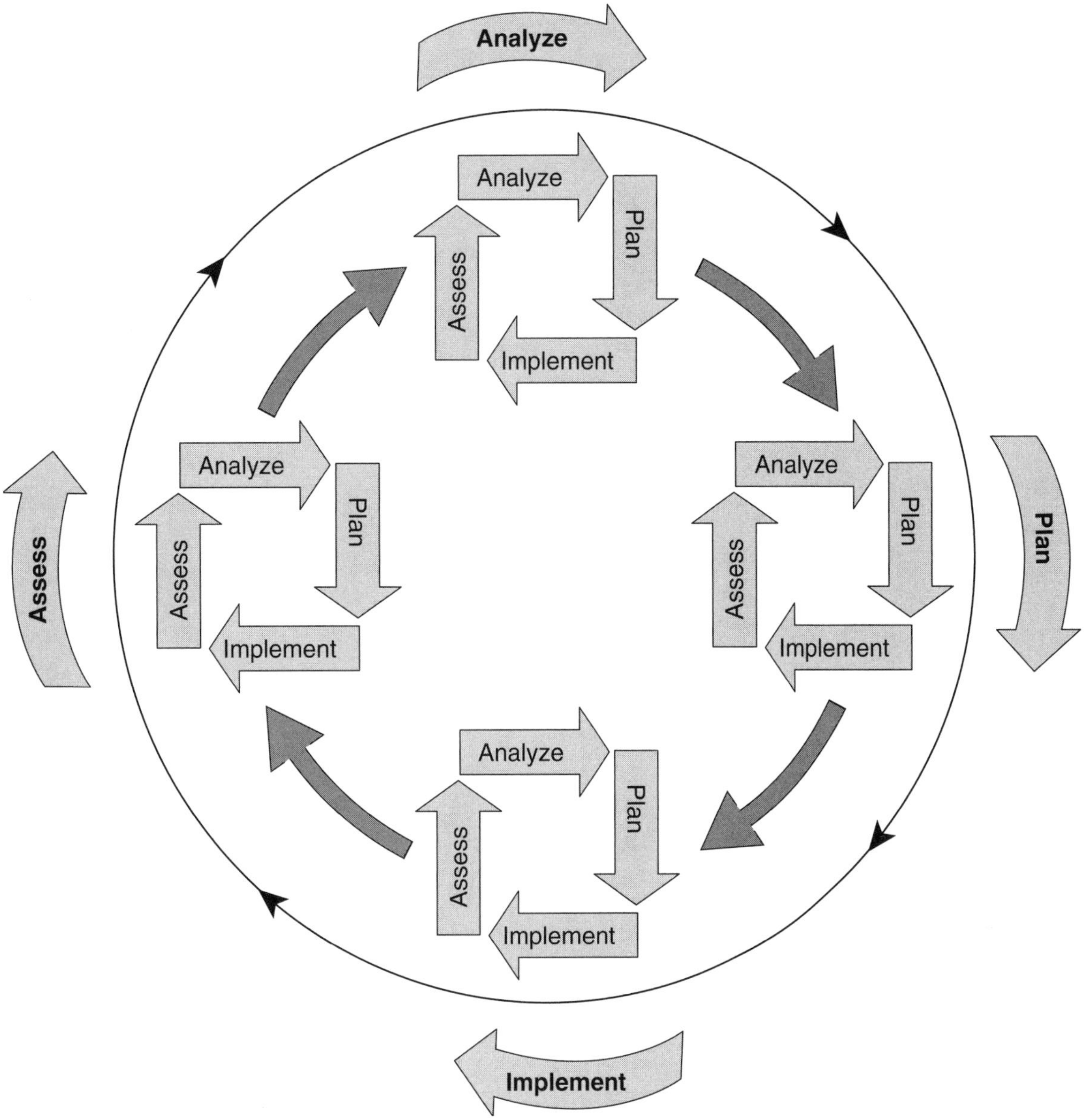

Copyright © 2006 by Corwin Press. All rights reserved. Reprinted from *The Data Guidebook for Teachers and Leaders: Tools for Continuous Improvement,* by Eileen Depka. Thousand Oaks, CA: Corwin Press, www.corwinpress.com. Reproduction authorized only for the local school site or nonprofit organization that has purchased this book.

The improvement cycle has both short- and long-term components. The larger plan may last three to five years. During that time, however, shorter cycles are also in the works, and progress of the plan's implementation is evaluated. The shorter cycles, which last up to a year, include analysis, planning, implementation, and assessment. To visualize the complexity of the improvement cycle, think of a double Ferris wheel. The outer wheel, as illustrated in Figure 1.3, is moving in slow rotation, whereas the inner wheels are spinning and continuing on their outer wheel path.

When a district begins to implement a continuous improvement cycle, an expectation needs to be set. The expectation is that all schools within the district actively implement the improvement cycle. Early in the improvement process, the process is an expectation. In time, the expectation is the process.

CLOSING THOUGHTS

Data are key to an effective cycle of continuous improvement. The focus is continuous growth in student achievement. Through data analysis and discussion, district weaknesses are identified. These provide the improvement targets. The use of an improvement cycle supplies a process by which plans can be created and implemented to support the elimination of identified challenges.

The chapters that follow suggest a variety of ways to represent, share, and use data within the continuous improvement cycle.

2

Data Collection

WHAT SHOULD BE COLLECTED?

Data collection is a foundational step in any improvement process. Some information is gathered regularly without much forethought. For example, state test data, demographic data, and school performance information are automatically gathered. Other measures may be available, but perhaps the data are not gathered. Although important, there may be no measurement tool currently in place. Making a conscious effort to identify and collect various types of data will assist districts in creating a well-rounded supply of information.

To determine the data to be collected, it helps to ask questions about your purpose. What do you want to know? Create a list of questions, the answers to which will give a complete picture of the school, its environment, and its students. You may ask the following questions: How do the students perform academically? How do they perform on standardized tests? What types of grades do they earn? Do they attend school on a regular basis? How is student behavior? What scores do the students earn on Advanced Placement, college aptitude, and achievement tests? How does the staff feel about the school? Is the school safe? How do parents feel about the school, its staff, and its policies? How do students who have been with the district since first grade perform compared with those who entered in later grades? When considering different subgroups, such as ethnic groups, does performance differ? What groups are doing well? How do they compare with groups outside of the school or district?

Each question points toward a data source that may currently exist or may need to be generated. Academic performance data probably currently exist in the form of standardized test results, classroom or report card grades, and district-level assessment results. Attitudinal data can be generated through surveys. Matching each question with one or more data sources can help to answer the questions previously stated.

A simple tool like the one in Figure 2.1 can help organize the brainstorming results. Its purpose is to link each question with achievement or attitudinal data that can answer the question. If no data source is available, needed sources or tools can be listed in the third column.

Consider the image of a photo collage. When creating such a collage about an individual, one wants a well-rounded look at various aspects of the individual's life. The goal is to bring out the person's personality through a series of snapshots. When looking at school data, the purpose is similar. What snapshots are needed to create a school collage? Figure 2.2 is a skeletal example of such a collage. It contains a variety of indictors related to school climate and performance. Included is a combination of statistical and attitudinal data. Any data placed on the form should have supporting evidence. Data should not be based on the opinion of those compiling the collage but rather based on the tools used to measure the areas listed within the collage.

CREATING A BALANCE

As data are collected, it is necessary to create a variety of balances. Items within the balance have been identified as a result of the brainstorming exercise completed when generating questions. The balance works to create a well-rounded collage. Missing an essential area could prove to mask an important piece of information. The individual units fit together to form the big picture—each is a piece of the pie. Figure 2.3 is an illustration of what the pie might include, using the information identified earlier. The size of each piece is determined by its level of importance in the situation. The amount of data collected and viewed should be equal to its importance in the continuous improvement process. Viewing the pieces in this format also helps groups determine the areas that need more data. If a piece is important, but there is little information currently available, it would be worthwhile to determine additional methods of data collection.

Creating a complete assessment picture for school evaluation purposes should include both standardized and district assessment data. Standardized assessments can help districts and states to compare themselves to others; however, there is no district control over test content. District assessment data provide a view of schools and classrooms within the district. How do schools or classrooms compare? How can the results be used to improve student achievement? The district measure is also closer to home. The district has control of the assessment content, and the teachers have control over methods used to improve performance on the measure.

When assessment results are evaluated to gain a multifaceted view of an individual, classroom assessment information needs to be added to the mix. Evaluations completed on a school or district level may include very limited if any individual classroom data. These data are typically not

Figure 2.1   Brainstorming Grid

What Do We Want to Know About Our School/District?

On the table below, brainstorm a list of questions to be answered. In the second column, list the data sources currently available that might generate answers. In the third column, list the needed but currently unavailable sources.

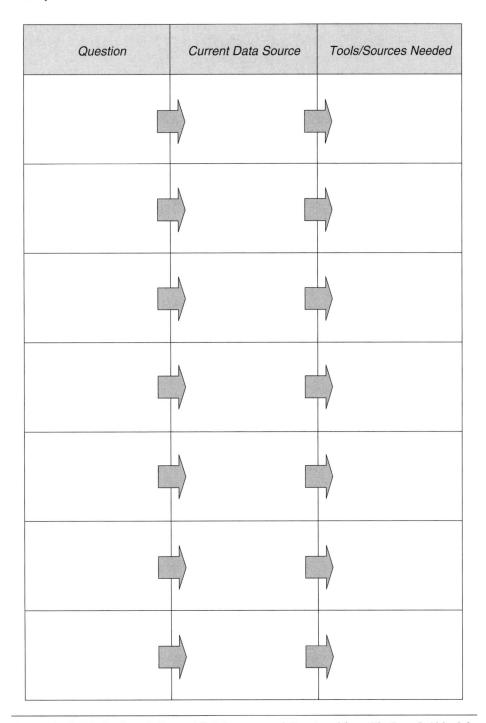

Question	Current Data Source	Tools/Sources Needed

Copyright © 2006 by Corwin Press. All rights reserved. Reprinted from *The Data Guidebook for Teachers and Leaders: Tools for Continuous Improvement,* by Eileen Depka. Thousand Oaks, CA: Corwin Press, www.corwinpress.com. Reproduction authorized only for the local school site or nonprofit organization that has purchased this book.

Figure 2.2   Data Collage Organizer

Data Collage for _____   From _____   Year _____

School or District

Strengths of Our School/District

According to Staff:

According to Students:

According to Parents:

Challenges of Our School/District

According to Staff:

According to Students:

According to Parents:

Activities Available to Our Students

Related to Academics	*Related to Sports*	*Related to Music*
Students Participating: _____ %	Students Participating: _____ %	Students Participating: _____ %

Attendance Rate

Our students attend school _____ % of the time.
Last year our students had a total of _____ absences.

Behavior

Last year _____ students were suspended.
Last year _____ students were expelled.
Last year _____ students had a disciplinary referral.

Advanced Placement (AP) Exams

Last year _____ students took one or more AP exams.
_____ % of those students received a grade of 3, 4, or 5.

Grades

_____ % of our students received passing grades for last semester.
_____ % of our students received one or more failing grades.

No Child Left Behind: Meeting Adequate Yearly Progress (AYP)

Reading: State benchmark is _____. Our school is at _____.
Math: State benchmark is _____. Our school is at _____.

Percentage of Students in Subgroups

Economically disadvantaged: _____ %

With disabilities: _____ %

English language learners: _____ %

By ethnicity:
_____ = _____ %
_____ = _____ %
_____ = _____ %
_____ = _____ %
_____ = _____ %

Class Size

Highest = _____

Lowest = _____

Average = _____

Academic Performance

Whole-Group Performance

Reading	Language Arts	Math	Science	Social Studies

Subgroup Performance: By Ethnicity

Reading	Language Arts	Math	Science	Social Studies

Subgroup Performance: By Disability

Reading	Language Arts	Math	Science	Social Studies

Subgroup Performance: By Economic Status

Reading	Language Arts	Math	Science	Social Studies

Subgroup Performance: By English Language Level

Reading	Language Arts	Math	Science	Social Studies

Copyright © 2006 by Corwin Press. All rights reserved. Reprinted from *The Data Guidebook for Teachers and Leaders: Tools for Continuous Improvement,* by Eileen Depka. Thousand Oaks, CA: Corwin Press, www.corwinpress.com. Reproduction authorized only for the local school site or nonprofit organization that has purchased this book.

Figure 2.3   Pieces of the Data Puzzle

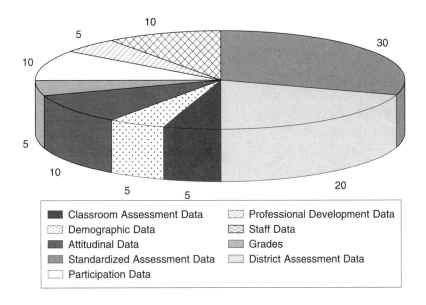

Copyright © 2006 by Corwin Press. All rights reserved. Reprinted from *The Data Guidebook for Teachers and Leaders: Tools for Continuous Improvement*, by Eileen Depka. Thousand Oaks, CA: Corwin Press, www.corwinpress.com. Reproduction authorized only for the local school site or nonprofit organization that has purchased this book.

collected at the school or district level and are not often comparable to assessments used in other classrooms. Classroom assessment, though, is a crucial part of the balance when assessing individual and classroom performance. Teachers should regularly collect and analyze classroom data to make instructional decisions. It is equally important for district assessment data to be made available to teachers. Analyzing and comparing their students' performance with the performance of other students throughout the district gives teachers a broader view of their students' performance level.

MUST-HAVE DATA

Data associated with the No Child Left Behind (NCLB) legislation are important to collect and analyze regularly—not simply when state or standardized test results are evaluated. It makes sense to know and understand progress in meeting NCLB goals. However, the legislation and the sanctions associated with failing to meet adequate yearly progress (AYP) should not be the driving force in inspiring long-term growth. Rather, the catalyst for change should be the desire to increase the achievement and understanding of all students. To enhance the achievement of all learners and meet AYP benchmarks, it is logical that specific types of data in standardized, district, and classroom assessment results be tracked.

Subgroup breakdowns of data furnish numbers that promote comparisons between groups in a given population. These disaggregations present information that is normally hidden within whole-group results. Generally, when preparing data, groups to consider include whole-group and subgroup populations. Subgroups should include racial or ethnic groups, economically disadvantaged students, English language learners, and students with disabilities. Another subgroup often viewed but not included in the NCLB accountability plan is gender.

To evaluate data, it first needs to be collected. Within the realm of standardized testing, this is not a problem. In a state testing situation, states provide systems with the disaggregated information needed to view subgroup performance. When other standardized tests are administered, disaggregated information can be purchased as a scoring option.

State tests are a yearly event for most students. These tests are an excellent data source for evaluating yearly growth, but they do not provide a constant source of information throughout the year.

When district assessments, often called common or benchmark assessments, are administered during the school year, disaggregations provide invaluable information for instructional planning and progress monitoring. It is nonproductive, even scary, to spend time evaluating student performance on state tests without another source of information to monitor progress throughout the year. Through the use of district assessments, and the monitoring of those results, schools can have hard data regarding the progress of their students. Educators need not keep their fingers crossed and hope for the best. Data collected throughout the year can be viewed, and plans to improve student achievement can be made, thereby affecting state test results. Key to collecting district information is access to a database or data warehouse in which results can be disaggregated. Subgroup results in district testing need to be analyzed as they are in state testing. If data are disaggregated to compare the subgroup results within and between schools, grade levels, and even teachers, the results can lead to crucial information. This data supply can help schools find areas of success. Is there a school, grade level, or teacher with a high level of success in one or more subgroups of students? What success strategies are these schools, grade levels, or teachers using? Can those strategies be shared with others in the school system? Not only can this information help teachers find the road to success, but it also has the potential of providing the map.

Regular analysis of subgroup results at the classroom level will have the greatest impact on student achievement. Classroom teachers, through their knowledge, performance, dedication, creativity, and perseverance, have always promoted understanding with an aim toward helping every student achieve. Arming teachers with data can help them focus their efforts. Being aware of which students or groups of students have a significant need will lead to specific plans to reach those learners. Implementing and evaluating the results of a new teaching strategy through the use of disaggregated data can give teachers the feedback they need to determine whether a strategy was successful. Consider the following sets of data.

Mr. Becher has given a math test to his sixth-grade students. After viewing individual results, he takes a few extra minutes to disaggregate the results. He studies the results and quickly learns that the average grade of his Hispanic students is quite a bit below the other ethnic subgroups in his classroom.

	Math Test 1
All students	79.52
Ethnicity: African American	81.71
Ethnicity: Hispanic	72.14
Ethnicity: White	84.14
Students with disabilities	78.33

Mr. Becher explains his findings to the other two sixth-grade teachers in his school and learns that both of them are experiencing success using manipulatives in math. He decides to give the strategy a try. The following chart shows the results of the next math test.

	Math Test 2
All students	82.04
Ethnicity: African American	81.71
Ethnicity: Hispanic	80.28
Ethnicity: White	84.14
Students with disabilities	82.33

The new test results indicate that students who were noticeably lower on the last test improved greatly on this assessment. Mr. Becher's Hispanic students made the greatest gains. He knows he doesn't have enough information yet to draw firm conclusions, but he feels that the use of manipulatives helped his students deepen their understanding of the math concepts he taught. He will continue to evaluate results and monitor the success of this and other strategies.

Classroom disaggregations do not need to take much time. If the assessment data are kept in a database that includes specific labels to identify subgroup information, numbers can be sorted and averaged in any way the teacher chooses. The value of the information far outweighs any drawback related to time. At a minimum, committing to complete disaggregations after cumulative classroom assessments will provide crucial information to the classroom teacher.

TOOLS: THE THREE "T'S"

To make data collection and organization efficient and effective, three tools are helpful.

Technology

Data reports on paper are valuable. Data points can be compared and conjectures developed about the reports. Often paper reports, like those often supplied with state test results, are a snapshot. Analysis involved in comparing reports and interpreting information is difficult and time-consuming. For example, if teachers want to measure student growth on their state test over a five-year period to see how it relates to the grades students are earning in school, a great deal of time would need to be spent finding and sorting the necessary reports. However, if the same information is kept on a computer in various databases, data can be compiled and sorted much more quickly. Computer technology is a necessity, and its use needs to be expected of anyone who evaluates student, school, or district performance.

If technology use is expected, then people need the appropriate technology to comply. Computer use is a key component in the data collection process. The use of computers to store, organize, and manipulate data leads to increased data collection by more individuals. The easier it is to access a computer, the more likely it is that more people will use them with an eye toward data analysis to increase student achievement. Providing the appropriate technology and the framework for data collection will increase the likelihood of a data-driven district.

Additional tools for data collection and analysis are available commercially. The data warehouse is a relatively new tool in education, but its use is expanding rapidly. A data warehouse helps to organize data so that it can be easily manipulated and used for educational decision making. A benefit of the data warehouse is that it can take minutes to get answers to detailed data inquiries. A drawback is that it can be quite expensive, often requiring a yearly fee.

Online assessment and evaluation programs are also readily available. These tools can save districts time by offering ready-made tests to evaluate and monitor student progress. Some include result analysis capabilities and even teaching suggestions to increase student understanding. Online assessment and progress monitoring programs provide districts with a service that is valuable in the school improvement process. These tools vary in cost but also can be quite expensive.

Training

Increased use of technology for data collection and analysis leads to a need for coordinated professional development. An expectation for data use must be accompanied by support and training, or the effort will expand only as far as users' current knowledge base.

Just as schools plan ahead for the needs of their students, they need to plan ahead for their employees. What new skills should all teachers have and use? How will the school or district support the acquisition of those skills? How and when will training be provided? What is an acceptable timeline? What expectations are there for use of the new skills?

Time

Time is a valuable commodity. Energy is equally as precious. Maintaining a productive balance between time and energy can have the greatest impact on the effects of staff development. Expecting staff to learn on their own will not guarantee that everyone is learning the same essential skills. There is also no control over the learning time frame. Learning new skills requires a fresh mind and committed, focused time. It is only possible to fit so much into a school day. Generate training options: Promote online learning and peer coaching; use faculty meeting time; institute early release days; or offer early morning, weekend, or summer opportunities. Brainstorm additional possibilities and then choose what works for your situation.

CLOSING THOUGHTS

To create a well-rounded view of a district, a list of questions that are tied to various facets of the system can be generated. Connecting the answers to the questions to existing or needed tools will identify data sources. Collection and organization of data at the district, school, and classroom levels provides a variety of information for analysis. A combination of multiple levels of data assists in forming a balanced view of district qualities and performance. Viewing data over time assists in identifying trends. Longitudinal data help to identify strengths and challenges. Although this compares different groups of students, it can clearly display grade-level trends. Comparing a student's individual growth over time can also create a valuable picture, which adds another view of student performance. Data disaggregations are necessary to view performance of school and district subgroups. Providing technology, training, and time is necessary for the effective collection and use of data.

3

Delving Into the Data

GETTING A CLOSER LOOK AT DATA

Time is valuable. Focused time spent viewing data is worth every minute. To make effective use of data, you need more than a superficial look. In-depth discussions surrounding various forms of data are a crucial component to the improvement cycle for improved student achievement. Through a data delve, an opportunity can be provided to view, analyze, discuss, and make recommendations based on hard evidence. With preparation and careful planning, a delve results in a successful and rewarding look into the strengths and challenges of a classroom, grade level, school, or district.

A delve is a gathering of individuals whose intent is to analyze data. Delves are an integral part of the ongoing process of continuous improvement. Getting a closer look at data provides the basis for informed decision making.

DEFINING A PURPOSE

The goal of the delve is to create a data-based profile with which questions will be raised, conjectures discussed, and ideas shared. The focus should not be placed on the data but on what the school or district intends to do with what they find. Therefore, the data delve should spend time with a variety of collected evidence to make suggestions or draw conclusions that will help in efforts to increase the level of success of all students. To use data effectively, it needs to be viewed as part of a cyclical process. The following illustration depicts this cycle.

Before putting the time and energy into a data delve, ask the following questions: What is the desired outcome of the experience? What do I want to accomplish? Am I researching a question? Am I evaluating achievement?

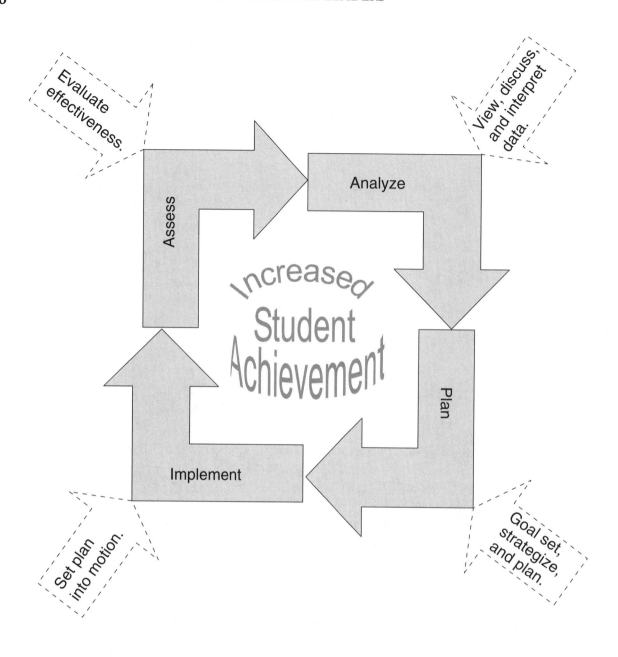

CREATING AN ATMOSPHERE OF ACCEPTANCE

Analyzing data is like getting on the scale in a doctor's office. Unless you know that you are going to be completely satisfied with the results, the event can be nerve-racking, even threatening. The thought of sharing the information with others is often not pleasing. Sharing test data can be equally as personal. Educators often dwell on the negative and downplay the positive. As a result, there can be an inherent fear when viewing data. If the test results are not as good as desired, excuses are manufactured in anticipation of blame being laid, even if blame was never the intent. As you may know, the blame game is both time-consuming and counter-productive. To have a productive experience, the anxiety associated with analyzing data needs to be eliminated. An atmosphere of trust increases the likelihood of a positive, productive experience.

If a delve is to be successful, all participants must be confident that the purpose is not to lay blame or build excuses. Rather, it is to analyze the results and paint a picture of the school or district: What do the data show? Participants should have no fear of retribution or finger pointing. The data are what they are. What is done or not done about the data is what matters.

How can administrators help teachers relax when viewing data? Be honest and build an atmosphere of acceptance and trust. Let everyone know that the goal is to analyze, not blame. What is, is. The plan is to analyze and interpret with an eye on improvement planning. The process is not and should never be about pointing fingers. It is about analysis followed by constructive conversation. The focus is continuous improvement and increased student understanding.

To further quell people's fears, be objective when discussing data. Preconceived notions do not apply unless supported by the data. Begin with an open mind and use language appropriate to the situation. Refer to data as "our results" not "your results." When discussing improvement planning, talk about what "we" will do to improve, not what "you" will do. Choosing words carefully will help to create an atmosphere of support and camaraderie. After all, everyone is working together to achieve a common goal: improved student achievement.

The tendency, when viewing assessment results, is to concentrate on the negative. To get a balanced view, time should be spent identifying the strengths as well as challenges of the school or district. Knowledge of strengths and weaknesses is important when developing a comprehensive look at student performance. Celebrating successes is rewarding; therefore, recognize successes and plan to eliminate challenges.

PLANNING AND IMPLEMENTING THE DATA DELVE

When organizing a data delve, preplanning and organization are as important as the delve itself. The goal is to use time effectively and efficiently during the process. Effective time management can be accomplished by following specific steps and answering some general questions.

Questions to Consider

What sources of data will be used?

A variety of data need to be chosen to create a well-rounded, data-based picture. Included could be a combination of standardized tests, district assessments, and attitudinal data. Figure 3.1 highlights some sources that may be considered. Review the various sources available to you. What will best meet your needs? For the best results, choose the data by matching it to the purpose of the delve.

Figure 3.1 Assessment Chart

Standardized Test Data	District Assessment Data	Attitudinal Data
Consider: • Results by content area • Results by subskill or standard • Item analyses • Disaggregations • Results by school • National/state comparisons • Longitudinal data	Consider: • Benchmark assessments • Grade-level assessments • District writing and math assessments • End-of-course assessments • Longitudinal data • Disaggregations	Consider: • Parent surveys • Student surveys • Teacher surveys • Technology surveys • Reflections • Anecdotal records • Longitudinal data

It is important to note that the saying "the more, the merrier" is not appropriate in this instance. Be selective about the data you choose for the delve. The data you select should relate to your goal. If the plan is to analyze student academic achievement, choose the sources that will give you the best all-around indications. It is important to provide enough data so that participants can have a good degree of confidence that their observations are accurate. Too much information at one data delve can overwhelm, confuse, and exhaust people. There certainly is a time and place to view it all, but the data should be viewed in segments to avoid data overload.

In what format should the data be presented?

Giving careful consideration to this question is crucial and directly related to the smooth running of the delve. Volumes of detailed information are often supplied to districts following a standardized or state test. Narrowing the information to fit the purpose, and identifying the pieces most crucial to the task at hand, will be helpful. Everyone is not comfortable with high-level math and statistics. As a result, all reports given to participants should be easy to interpret or explain. It would be helpful to accompany a report being used with an explanation of how to read the report. Both written and verbal explanations can be used and are best augmented with a time for questions and clarifications. More information about reporting data can be found in Chapters 4–7.

Often standardized test reports include multiple pieces of information on the same page. If it is possible to pull the essential information from the report and place it on a chart or a graph, valuable time will be saved. Examples of easy-to-read report formats appear in Chapter 4. Use manufactured standardized reports when they are useful but not overwhelming.

What levels of data should be considered?

Standardized test data typically are reported on three levels: student, school, and district. The levels of data used at a delve depend on the purpose of the delve. When looking at school and district performance, it makes sense to have school and district data as well as at least one outside comparison, such as state or national results.

If the goal is to better meet the needs of specific individuals, individual student data are needed. The purpose of individual performance data is to analyze individual strengths and challenges and to set individual goals. Individual student data can be available at a data delve but is not typically the primary focus. Looking at the big picture comes first.

For a district delve, collect and organize data for a variety of grade levels, making sure that there is representation from primary, intermediate, and secondary schools.

How can information be organized for efficiency?

Many pieces of information will need to be duplicated and compiled for each delve participant. Advance preparation saves time and assists in the flow of the event. If possible, color code data so that specific information is readily located and easy to distinguish from other sources. To avoid paper shuffling and distributing during the delve, place data in folders or binders for each participant. If possible, each person should have access to district data, as well as data that apply to their particular school or situation.

Who will participate in the delve?
Do I have a balanced representation?

Gathering input from a variety of individuals holding different positions in the school or district is helpful when viewing the data. Consider including teachers at multiple grade levels, staff members who teach specialty areas, as well as school and district administrators. Placing participants in groups of four to six people will help encourage discussion. Mixed groups are beneficial because they provide multiple perspectives when sharing thoughts and observations. Groups might also participate as school teams. Parents and students can have valuable input as well. Providing an opportunity for them to view data at an alternate time is suggested.

How much time is needed?

Viewing and analyzing data take time, especially when the processes are new to those involved. To make efficient use of time, each new or unique form used to represent data needs to be explained. Explain forms as they are to be used. The groups can refer to their own copies of the reports, while you display them on a large screen. Avoid explaining all forms at once. This tends to confuse and overwhelm participants. An effective pattern to use and repeat is the explain-view-discuss pattern.

When developing an approximate time frame for the pattern, allow one to two minutes per explanation and fifteen minutes per page for viewing and discussing. Multiple pages of the same type of report can be distributed at the same time. For example, a report of average scaled scores reported by content area and skills tested might be distributed for all content areas simultaneously. Various grade levels might be viewed independently of one another to avoid confusion.

If a large block of time is available, scheduled breaks are imperative. Participants will be more engaged if given the opportunity to refresh. If data are viewed in several small chunks of time, be conscious of using an appropriate amount of data and recording thoughts and ideas so that they are not forgotten before the next session.

Figure 3.2 can be used to assist in the planning process. Figure 3.3 is an example of a completed delve worksheet.

During the Delve

While the delve is in progress, you should keep time and introduce data reports. While groups are discussing reports, it is important to be available to provide explanations and clarification. Floating between groups will help determine group progress. Time allotments need to be flexible. If some data require less time to view, move on. If more time is needed, adjust the schedule, keeping in mind how much time you will need to allow groups to view all of the reports. When working with larger groups, it is difficult to keep a pace that will keep all participants happy. Some will need more time, some less time. Conducting time checks works well. Stop the group about two minutes before the scheduled time is up and ask them how they are doing. If they need additional time, offer more time, perhaps an additional ten minutes. Also, let participants know that it will be necessary to move on when time expires, but tell them they can have access to earlier data throughout the delve.

Before introducing each new section of data, take time to ask for discoveries made related to the previous reports. This does not need to be a report from each group but rather observations from those who want to share. To encourage sharing, ask the following questions: Who would be willing to share one thing that your group noticed? Were any particular strengths pinpointed? Where do the challenges seem to lie?

To promote the smooth operation of the delve, make sure all participants are able to share their thoughts. Try to prevent one person from monopolizing the discussion. If it appears that someone is speaking more than others, join the group temporarily and ask other members to share their thoughts. Stay in the group until it appears that others are being given the opportunity to contribute to the discussion.

Focus Questions and Organizational Tools

Making available a variety of graphic organizers is important because participants need to record their thoughts and observations while viewing data. As thoughts, opinions, and questions arise, individuals should be encouraged to record them immediately. If ideas aren't scripted as they arrive, they are likely to be forgotten. Delve participants can be given an organizational tool for each type of data being viewed. Participants can later compare forms to see if there are similarities between

Figure 3.2   Data Delve Planning Worksheet

Data Delve Planning Worksheet

Date _____   Time _____   Location _____

Goal:
Delve Participants:
Data to Be Used (color code if possible):
Organizational Tools Needed:
Agenda/Time Allotments:
Follow-Up:

Copyright © 2006 by Corwin Press. All rights reserved. Reprinted from *The Data Guidebook for Teachers and Leaders: Tools for Continuous Improvement,* by Eileen Depka. Thousand Oaks, CA: Corwin Press, www.corwinpress.com. Reproduction authorized only for the local school site or nonprofit organization that has purchased this book.

Figure 3.3   Data Delve Planning Worksheet Example

Data Delve Planning Worksheet

Date _____   Time _____   Location _____

Goal:

View and analyze data to discover school and district strengths and challenges. Plan potential steps to improve student achievement and set potential goal areas.

Delve Participants:

Principals—Amy Smith, Jason Grey, Fred Myer

Teachers—Alan Major, Brenda Walden, Jill Trem, Alan Nolan, Rita Alben, Jenna Freed

District administrators—John Swan, Wendy Hamprin

Data to Be Used (color code if possible):

Fourth-grade longitudinal data for state test, school, and district (blue)

Eighth-grade longitudinal data for state test, school, and district (green)

Tenth-grade longitudinal data for state test, school, and district (yellow)

All district writing assessment data for school and district (pink)

Organizational Tools Needed:

Data Delve Collective Data Reflection

Data Delve Individual Source Reflection Worksheet—one for each data source

---

Agenda/Time Allotments:

30 minutes	View fourth-grade longitudinal test data by content area
15 minutes	Discuss findings
30 minutes	View eighth-grade longitudinal test data by content area
15 minutes	Discuss findings
30 minutes	View tenth-grade longitudinal test data by content area
15 minutes	Break
15 minutes	Discuss findings
30 minutes	View district writing data
45 minutes	Discuss and compare collective findings

Follow-Up:

Share results with administrators and teachers not in attendance.

Collectively decide what insights data have given and suggest a course of action with school improvement planning.

their discoveries. For example, if one graphic organizer is used for fourth-grade data and another for eighth grade, comparisons can be made to identify commonalities between the two. Figure 3.4 is an example of one tool that can be used. The purpose is to have participants record their observations by content area. This graphic organizer helps promote discussion about strengths and challenges within and between subject areas. Figure 3.5 is a completed version of the same tool. When analyzing longitudinal data, the organizer found in Figure 3.6 can be used. Figure 3.7 is a completed example of Figure 3.6. When groups are given a set of data to analyze and a graphic organizer to complete, the discussion that takes place greatly affects the success of the delve.

Providing an assortment of focus questions is beneficial. Whereas graphic organizers provide an organized form to record conversations, focus questions work as discussion starters. Figure 3.8 contains a list of possible focus questions. Depending on your preference, you may want to select a specific question on which to focus for each portion of the delve. Additional data-specific questions are located in Chapters 4 and 5.

Analysis and Interpretation of Data

As charts, graphs, and various reports are viewed, participants will see trends, questions will be raised, and suggestions will be shared. This is the beginning of the most valuable purpose for the delve. Through discussion of the data, hypotheses are voiced and pathways for improvement are established. Data delve discussions plant the seed that eventually grows into an improvement plan or supports an existing plan. When need is identified through data, a clear focus is created for further growth and development.

Products and Planning

Products of the delve include any organizational tools that are used during the delve. The notes that were taken provide teams with a record of their findings.

Planning for the future should be an expectation with any delve. An important step involves answering questions such as the following: Does this information support the focus of our school goals? What will we do with what we have learned?

The answers to these questions are the underlying theme of the delve: They get back to the purpose. Participants look at data as part of a continuous improvement process. As a result, before the delve is finished, groups should discuss and plan how the newfound information will be used within that process. Figure 3.9 is an organizational tool meant to help with this task. Providing an opportunity to complete the form by the end of the delve ensures that it is finished. To monitor and support progress, a follow-up meeting should be scheduled.

Figure 3.4 Data Delve Collective Reflection Worksheet

Data Delve Collective Reflection Worksheet

Content Area	Strengths	Challenges	Suggestions/Questions
Reading			
Language Arts			
Mathematics			
Science			
Social Studies			

Data Sources Viewed	Grade Level(s)	Years of Source Data

Copyright © 2006 by Corwin Press. All rights reserved. Reprinted from *The Data Guidebook for Teachers and Leaders: Tools for Continuous Improvement*, by Eileen Depka. Thousand Oaks, CA: Corwin Press, www.corwinpress.com. Reproduction authorized only for the local school site or nonprofit organization that has purchased this book.

Figure 3.5   Data Delve Collective Reflection Worksheet Example

Data Delve Collective Reflection Worksheet

Content Area	Strengths	Challenges	Suggestions/Questions
Reading	Reading results are comparatively positive and continue to rise on a yearly basis.		Continue the efforts we put into reading. They appear to be working.
Language Arts	Sentence structure, mechanics, and grammar	Writing	Look into increasing writing opportunities for all students.
Mathematics	Students seem to do comparatively well with basic calculations.	There appears to be significant weaknesses in problem solving, reasoning, and communication.	Share math results with others. What might we do to improve?
Science		Varied by grade level.	Compare curriculum to what is being tested. Does it match?
Social Studies		Reading and interpreting information causes some problems.	

Data Sources Viewed	Grade Level(s)	Years of Source Data
Longitudinal data for state test, school, and district	Fourth	1999–2004
Longitudinal data for state test, school, and district	Eighth	1999–2004
Longitudinal data for state test, school, and district	Tenth	1999–2004
All district writing assessment data, school, and district	Grades 2–12	2002–2004

Figure 3.6   Longitudinal Data Worksheet

Longitudinal Data Worksheet

Complete the table for each year of data provided. Use a separate table for each grade level and test.

Draw a circle around the lowest score for each year.

Draw a square around the highest score for each year.

Years	Language Arts	Reading	Mathematics	Science	Social Studies

Data Source	Grade Level

What Do You Notice About the Results?

Strengths	Challenges	Questions	Comparisons to Other Data Sources

Copyright © 2006 by Corwin Press. All rights reserved. Reprinted from *The Data Guidebook for Teachers and Leaders: Tools for Continuous Improvement*, by Eileen Depka. Thousand Oaks, CA: Corwin Press, www.corwinpress.com. Reproduction authorized only for the local school site or nonprofit organization that has purchased this book.

Figure 3.7   Longitudinal Data Worksheet Example

Longitudinal Data Worksheet

Complete the table for each year of data provided. Use a separate table for each grade level and test.

Draw a circle around the lowest score for each year.

Draw a square around the highest score for each year.

	Percentage of Students Proficient or Higher				
Years	*Language Arts*	*Reading*	*Mathematics*	*Science*	*Social Studies*
2000–2001	68%	88%	45%	56%	78%
2001–2002	70%	92%	40%	75%	78%
2002–2003	70%	90%	38%	82%	80%
2003–2004	82%	92%	40%	85%	82%

Data Source	*Grade Level*
State Test	4

What Do You Notice About the Results?		
Strengths	*Challenges*	*Questions*
For all of the past four years, students have had top scores in reading.	During the past four years, math scores have been lower than any other content area.	Why are the math scores so much lower than scores in other content areas?
		Is it true across all schools in the district?
		Is the test different in math?
		What should we do about what we see?

Comparisons to Other Data Sources
Math scores are consistently lower across all grade levels tested.
Reading scores are consistently higher in the district.

Figure 3.8 Discussion Strarters

Discussion Starters

Questions About the Data	Questions About Needs	Questions About the Future
• Does anything confuse you about the data?	• What other sources of information do you need to get a balanced view of your school?	• With whom would you like to share the observations of your group?
• Does anything surprise you about the data?	• What form do you prefer when reviewing data (graphs, charts, tables, reports)?	• What do you think should be done about what you see?
• What do you see that is worth celebrating?	• During the delve, is there anything that would have made it easier for your group to work?	• Where might there be room for improvement?
• When comparing student performance results at different grade levels, what do you notice?		• How does student performance compare from this year to last?
• How does your school compare to district performance?	**Questions About Data Sources**	• Is there an improvement strategy that you would suggest?
• When looking at trend data, what do you notice? Is there a difference between content areas?	• What data sources were most valuable to your group?	• Do you have any suggestions regarding the school improvement process?
• How does the performance of subgroups compare with that of the entire population?	• Which sources can potentially have a greater impact on student achievement?	

Additional Discussion Starters

Copyright © 2006 by Corwin Press. All rights reserved. Reprinted from *The Data Guidebook for Teachers and Leaders: Tools for Continuous Improvement*, by Eileen Depka. Thousand Oaks, CA: Corwin Press, www.corwinpress.com. Reproduction authorized only for the local school site or nonprofit organization that has purchased this book.

Figure 3.9   Delve Follow-Up Plans

Delve Follow-Up Plans

Team Members:

School:

Key Findings From the Delve:	
How will finding be shared with other key stakeholders? Be specific.	
How will the findings be used to support the continuous improvement process?	

What specific actions will be taken as a result of the delve?	**By whom?**	**In what time frame?**

Copyright © 2006 by Corwin Press. All rights reserved. Reprinted from *The Data Guidebook for Teachers and Leaders: Tools for Continuous Improvement,* by Eileen Depka. Thousand Oaks, CA: Corwin Press, www.corwinpress.com. Reproduction authorized only for the local school site or nonprofit organization that has purchased this book.

Analyze

Continuous Improvement Planning

Continuous improvement planning is necessary to support increased student achievement. Setting and attaining any goal is part of a process. Making data an integral part of that process helps districts see what is working and what is not. Data help fine-tune plans and shed light on the effectiveness of school and district efforts. The time and energy spent on data analysis is well worth it when those efforts are directly connected to continuous improvement planning.

If your district has a continuous improvement planning process in place, great. If not, consider starting this process as part of your data delve:

- Analyze your data.
- Research strategies.
- Identify strategies that will have an impact on student learning in the greatest areas of district need.
- Develop and implement a plan to learn and use the strategies.
- Determine how the plan will be assessed and assess its successfulness.

Then start all over again. Additional thought regarding continuous improvement planning can be found in Chapter 1.

Figure 3.10   Data Delve Reflection

List two things you found interesting.	Share one question you have.	What do you want to tell the delve organizer?
1.		
2.		

Copyright © 2006 by Corwin Press. All rights reserved. Reprinted from *The Data Guidebook for Teachers and Leaders: Tools for Continuous Improvement*, by Eileen Depka. Thousand Oaks, CA: Corwin Press, www.corwinpress.com. Reproduction authorized only for the local school site or nonprofit organization that has purchased this book.

Reflection

It is beneficial to have a three- to five-minute reflective opportunity at the end of a delve. Reflection serves two purposes. First, it provides you with feedback on the effectiveness of the event and the follow-up that may need to be completed in the future. Second, it provides delve participants with time to process the activities of the day and organize their thoughts. The reflection can easily take the place of a typical evaluation, and the information can potentially be more meaningful. The reflection can be as simple as the example in Figure 3.10.

CLOSING THOUGHTS

The data delve is an essential component of any school or district improvement process. Preplanning can result in an effective data viewing experience. Through the identification of strengths and challenges, a focus is established that can suggest a pathway toward improved student achievement. Data are the catalyst that create a sense of urgency. Growth and change results as ideas are born, strategies identified, and plans outlined. The data delve is a primary component in the path toward increased student achievement.

4

Standardized and State Test Data

Volumes of data are often supplied following the administration of standardized and state tests. It is necessary to dig through the results and find key pieces of information for your district. Decide which reports provide data aligned with your school improvement efforts. Distinguish between which pieces are essential and which are simply nice to know. Narrowing the number of reports you deal with will make the task more manageable. All other information is still available to you should it be needed to answer specific questions as they arise.

REPORTING DATA

To understand data, it is helpful to experiment with ways of reporting it. Creating various charts and visual representations of the data can aid with interpretation. Comparing the same data in different formats can help you decide which representations are the easiest to view and evaluate.

Figure 4.1 contains data from a standardized achievement test. It shows the performance of a district for five consecutive years in mathematics. Charted information often takes longer to study and interpret due to the large amount of numbers. To better interpret data in charts, you can highlight numbers. For example, in each subtest, the lowest number can be highlighted in one color, the highest in another. The results can then be discussed and interpreted.

Placing chart data in a graph provides a visual representation of the data. This picture can make the data easier to interpret. Patterns can be recognized, interpreted, and discussed. The graphs in Figures 4.2 and 4.3 are representations of the same scores. Looking at a variety of graphs

Figure 4.1   District Math Results Chart

District State Test Math Results: Percentage of Correct Responses					
Computation	52	53	52	67	75
Estimation	52	58	57	61	75
Measurement	50	51	52	66	72
Geometry/Spatial Sense	47	53	57	68	72
Data/Statistics/Probability	42	45	55	62	61
Problem Solving/Reasoning	50	48	52	68	72
Communication	60	66	57	70	84
Subtest Objective	00	01	02	03	04
Subtest average	**50**	**53**	**55**	**66**	**73**

Figure 4.2   State Test Results Bar Graph by Year

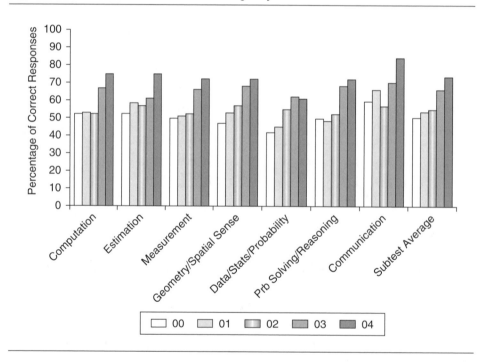

connected to the same data can help you choose which best meets the needs of those who will be viewing them. The purpose of Figures 4.2 and 4.3 is to help viewers visualize the differences in district, yearly state test scores in math, with an emphasis on growth over time. Which graph might be the easiest for a group to interpret? The line graph clearly illustrates that student performance in 2004 reflects all-time high scores in nearly every tested area. The bar graph, however, does a better job of showing dramatic average growth over the five-year period.

Figure 4.3   State Test Results Line Graph by Year

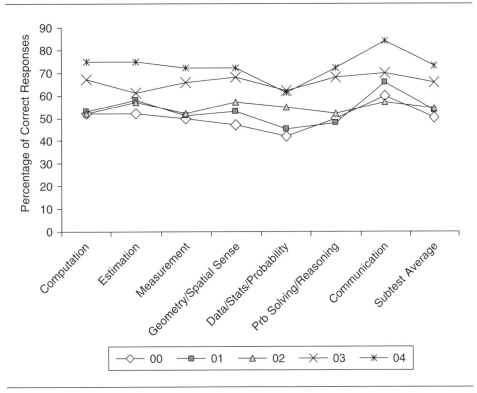

The same information can be graphed differently to create another picture. Figures 4.4 and 4.5 place the emphasis on a comparison of performance by subskill. The purpose of this representation is to analyze and compare strengths and challenges within mathematics. What can be said about student performance in the various subskills? One observation might be that the district appears to have increasing scores in the area of communication, which, in four separate years, also received the highest score. In this instance, the bar graph is clearly easier to interpret. The line graph appears cluttered and confusing. Experimenting with various types of graphs will help to identify the best form for your purpose. Complex graphs are much easier to interpret when printed in color.

If the graph is not labeled with exact data points, provide the charted information along with the graph. The information needs to be available to make detailed comparisons. Providing both on a regular basis addresses the personal preferences and learning styles of the viewers.

Other pieces of valuable information to make available include the size of the population tested and the time of year the tests were administered.

Disaggregated views of the previous data are necessary to get a deeper understanding of the results. Other data should include school, classroom, and perhaps individual performance. The extent of the details would be defined by the current purpose of the data review team. Subgroup performance at the district level should also be evaluated. More information on subgroups and disaggregations can be found in Chapter 2. More information on data analysis and interpretation is located in Chapter 3.

Figure 4.4   State Test Results Bar Graph by Standard

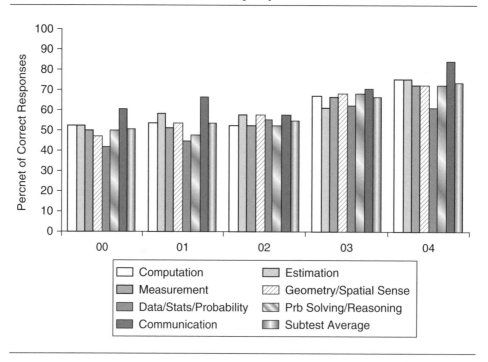

Figure 4.5   State Test Results Line Graph by Standard

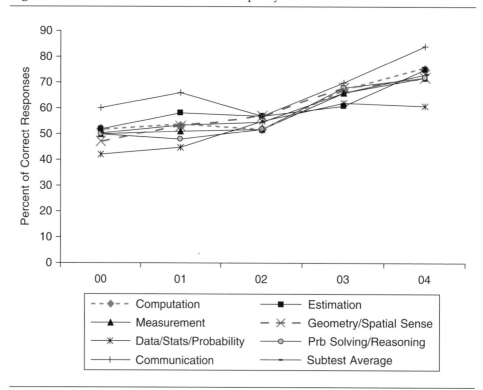

COMPARING RESPONSE TYPES

Many standardized tests include two categories of questions: selected response and constructed response. Selected response questions, often referred to as multiple-choice questions, require students to choose from a bank of provided answers.

Example

Mrs. Labas is deciding what she should wear to work today. She has 2 skirts, 4 sweaters, and 3 pairs of shoes to choose from. How many combinations are available to her?

   A. 9 combinations
   B. 21 combinations
   C. 24 combinations
   D. None of the above

Constructed response items require students to manufacture an answer. They might be asked to create a picture, chart, or graph. The response might include a written explanation of a procedure or a written interpretation of information provided in the test booklet. The types of responses required differ from question to question. Constructed response items require an application of knowledge often incorporating communication skills.

Example

Devin was asked to create a 3-shape pattern using only 1 shape from each box. Draw every possible pattern Devin could create. Explain your answer.

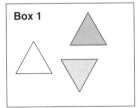 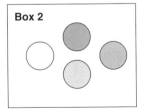 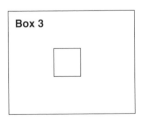

Selected response items are worth one point. Constructed response answers can have increased point value. These questions are quite different in their expectations of students. Student involvement in identifying an answer is also dissimilar. As a result, it can be enlightening to look at student performance by comparing selected and constructed response data.

Comparisons are not always provided and may need to be created using item analysis results. Separate pages may need to be compared and combined. Subtest or content area averages may need to be located. The charts in Figures 4.6 and 4.7 provide an illustration.

In their current form, the data are difficult to compare. To make the data easier to interpret, first turn the points earned into percentages of points earned. To help with the comparisons, list both numbers as percentages on the same chart. See Figure 4.8.

To further assist in the interpretation of these numbers, a horizontal bar chart can be effective (see Figure 4.9). In this representation, it is clear that students appear to be experiencing a higher level of success with selected response items on their standardized test.

Figure 4.6   Selected Response Results

Selected Response Results	
Subtest Objective	Percentage Correct
Computation	86
Estimation	85
Measurement	95
Geometry/Spatial Sense	81
Data/Statistics/Probability	82
Problem Solving/Reasoning	87
Communication	80
Subtest Average	85

Figure 4.7   Constructed Response Results

Constructed Response Results		
Subtest Objective	Points Possible	Points Earned
Computation	12	7
Estimation	14	8
Measurement	12	6
Geometry/Spatial Sense	10	6
Data/Statistics/Probability	8	5
Problem Solving/Reasoning	6	3
Communication	10	4
All Subtests	**Total = 72**	**Average = 6**

Figure 4.8   Selected/Constructed Combined Chart

Subtest Objective	Selected Response Percentage Correct	Constructed Response Percentage of Points Earned
Computation	86	58
Estimation	85	57
Measurement	95	50
Geometry/Spatial Sense	81	60
Data/Statistics/Probability	82	63
Problem Solving/Reasoning	87	50
Communication	80	40
Subtest Average	85	54

Figure 4.9   Selected/Constructed Combined Graph

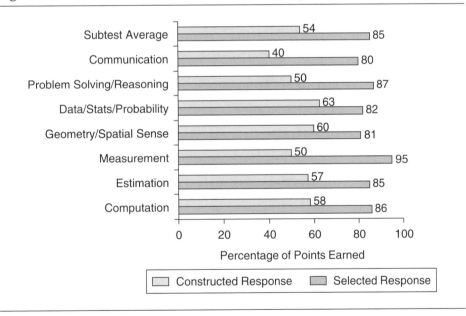

Charts like these are beneficial at the school and district levels. Interesting results can also surface when comparing performance differences between schools.

ITEM ANALYSIS

An item analysis provides performance information on each question of an assessment. The item analysis can offer a great deal of information,

Figure 4.10   Selected Response Item Analysis Chart

Constructed Response Item Analysis						
Question	A	B	C	D	E	No Answer
1	24%	60%	10%	3%	3%	0%
2	24%	23%	30%	23%	0%	0%
3	22%	30%	38%	0%	3%	7%
4	2%	90%	2%	0%	3%	3%

NOTE: Shading indicates the correct response.

depending on what is made available. For each selected response question, the report reveals the answer choices available and the percentage of students marking each answer. The correct answer choice is also indicated. An abbreviated example of the type of information found in an item analysis is contained in Figure 4.10.

Although the format varies, information in the reports will be consistent. Time spent analyzing these reports is extremely valuable, especially when you have access to the test questions.

When viewing the item analysis, certain elements should be looked at consistently. The following list of questions will help generate discussions. The first question in each set can be answered using only the item analysis. If test question items are available for viewing, the second question should be answered as well.

On which items did the students do extremely well?

After viewing the question: Why were students highly successful answering these questions?

On which questions was an incorrect response chosen more often than a correct response?

After viewing the question: Why might that be the case?

Are there questions that students did not attempt to answer?

After viewing the question: Why might this be the case?

Are there questions with evenly balanced responses across items?

After viewing the question: Why might this have occurred?

On which items did only a small number of students answer correctly?

After viewing the question: Why might this be the case?

The reason for studying the item analysis and viewing the test items is not to find excuses for a performance but to plan for the future. Determining the types of questions that students are answering incorrectly can be enlightening. Is reading an issue? Realizing that directions weren't followed or that the last question on a page is often skipped or that the final questions in a section are regularly not answered are pieces of information that can point teachers to test-taking strategies. If serious gaps in knowledge are discovered, holes in the curriculum can be addressed. On occasion, you might even find a bad question or two.

An item analysis for constructed response questions is slightly different. It is typically based on points earned compared to points available. It is also valuable if information is supplied regarding questions not attempted or undecipherable (refer to Figure 4.11).

When viewing these results, some additional questions can be asked:

- What percentage of the students earned the highest point value possible?
- Do students regularly not attempt an answer?
- Which questions are unable to be read?
- Are students regularly attempting answers but receiving no points?
- *After viewing the questions:* Are there specific types of questions that students are less likely to answer?
- *After viewing the questions:* Are there skills not related to the content area that students need to create a successful response?
- *After viewing the questions:* What else did you notice when viewing the item analyses?

Item analyses can be particularly important at the school level. If test booklets are available and identical tests are not used yearly, get the questions into the hands of the teachers. For teachers to value state testing, they need to receive and analyze results with the test in hand. This is not meant to encourage teaching to the test but rather to gather an in-depth

Figure 4.11   Constructed Response Item Analysis

Question	0 Point	1 Point	2 Points	3 Points	4 Points	No Answer	Unable to Be Read
1	0 10%	1 15%	2 25%	3 40%	4	5%	5%
2	0 3%	1 7%	2 50%	3 28%	4	7%	5%
3	0 20%	1 10%	2 40%	3	4	25%	5%
4	0 10%	1 15%	2 5%	3 35%	4 15%	15%	5%

NOTE: Shading indicates largest point value available.

understanding of what students know, to find what they can do with what they know, and to identify what they clearly struggle with. Difficulties may be connected to content, test-taking skills, confidence levels, readability, application skills, or a number of other causes. Given the chance to use their expertise, teachers will find acceptable and effective paths to improved student achievement. Without the time and ability to analyze strengths and challenges item by item, it will be more difficult to have a direct impact in the classroom.

PROMOTING ANALYSIS AND DISCUSSION

As teams work to evaluate and understand data, various questions arise. Some questions are gold mines when it comes to promoting total staff involvement and discussion. The following questions surfaced at a recent data delve: Is there a connection between standardized test performance and school grades? Could test performance be an indicator of school success? These questions were found to generate high interest. Without data, educators can only speculate on the answers.

The delve decided to compare student scale scores on a standardized test with students' most recent report card grades. Comparisons were made by content area in language arts, mathematics, science, and social studies. Student scores were entered into a database, which was no small undertaking. By the time the project got rolling, thousands of scores had been manually entered into the computer.

Students were ranked in the database from lowest to highest scale score by subject area. Figure 4.12 shows an example of the simple database organization.

Graphs were generated to provide pictures of the results. After an initial viewing, teachers decided that additional information would be valuable. They asked for student absences and discipline referrals to be added to the database and for graphs to be reprinted. Figure 4.13 reflects the changes in the database.

Individual graphs were created with twenty students per page. Approximately twenty pages of students were printed per content area per school. One long graph was created by taping all twenty of the individual pages together. Please see the image below for a miniature example.

Figure 4.14 shows examples of the first and last pages of the social studies graph. As you will see, each bar represents a student and is color coded to reflect the student's course grade. Discipline referrals and absences are indicated beneath each bar. Take a moment to study Figure 4.14. What do you notice? What would you like to know more about?

Figure 4.12   Grade/Score Comparison

Name	Course Grades	Scale Scores
Joel	D	548
Casey	F	629
Rachel	F	653
Krystal	D	659
Norbert	D	664
Max	B	667
Carl	C	676
Joelle	C	676
Michelle	F	677
Jennifer	C–	678
Dylan	C	678
Spence	B–	679

Figure 4.13   Discipline Referrals, Absences, Grade, and Scale Score Comparison Chart

Name	Discipline Referrals/Absences	Course Grades	Scale Scores
Joel	d34 a45	D	548
Casey	d0 a11	F	629
Rachel	d4 a44	F	653
Krystal	d22 a45	D	659
Norbert	d20 a26	D	664
Max	d2 a1	B	667
Carl	d7 a21	C	676
Joelle	d23 a35	C	676
Michelle	d22 a33	F	677
Jennifer	d12 a15	C–	678
Dylan	d1 a8	C	678
Spence	d0 a2	B–	679

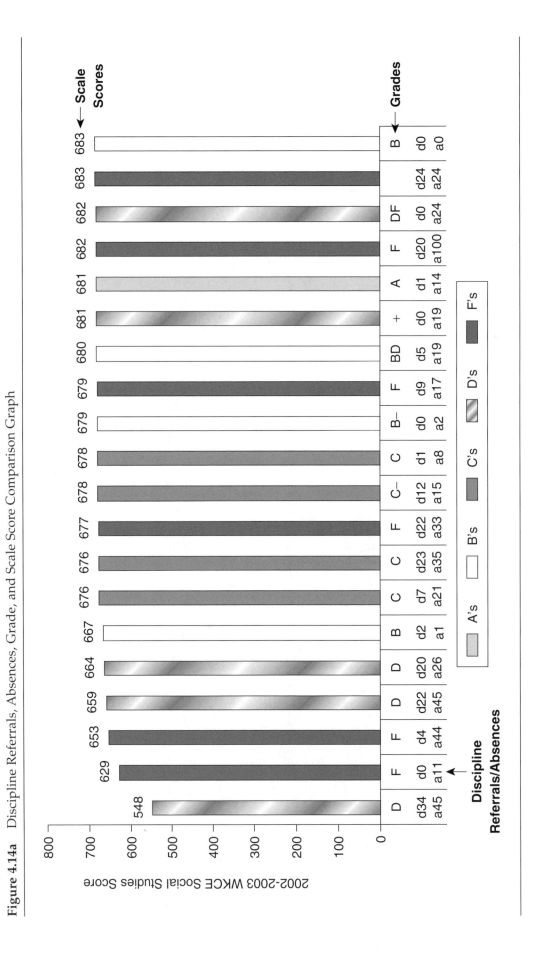

Figure 4.14a Discipline Referrals, Absences, Grade, and Scale Score Comparison Graph

Figure 4.14b Discipline Referrals, Absences, Grade, and Scale Score Comparison Graph

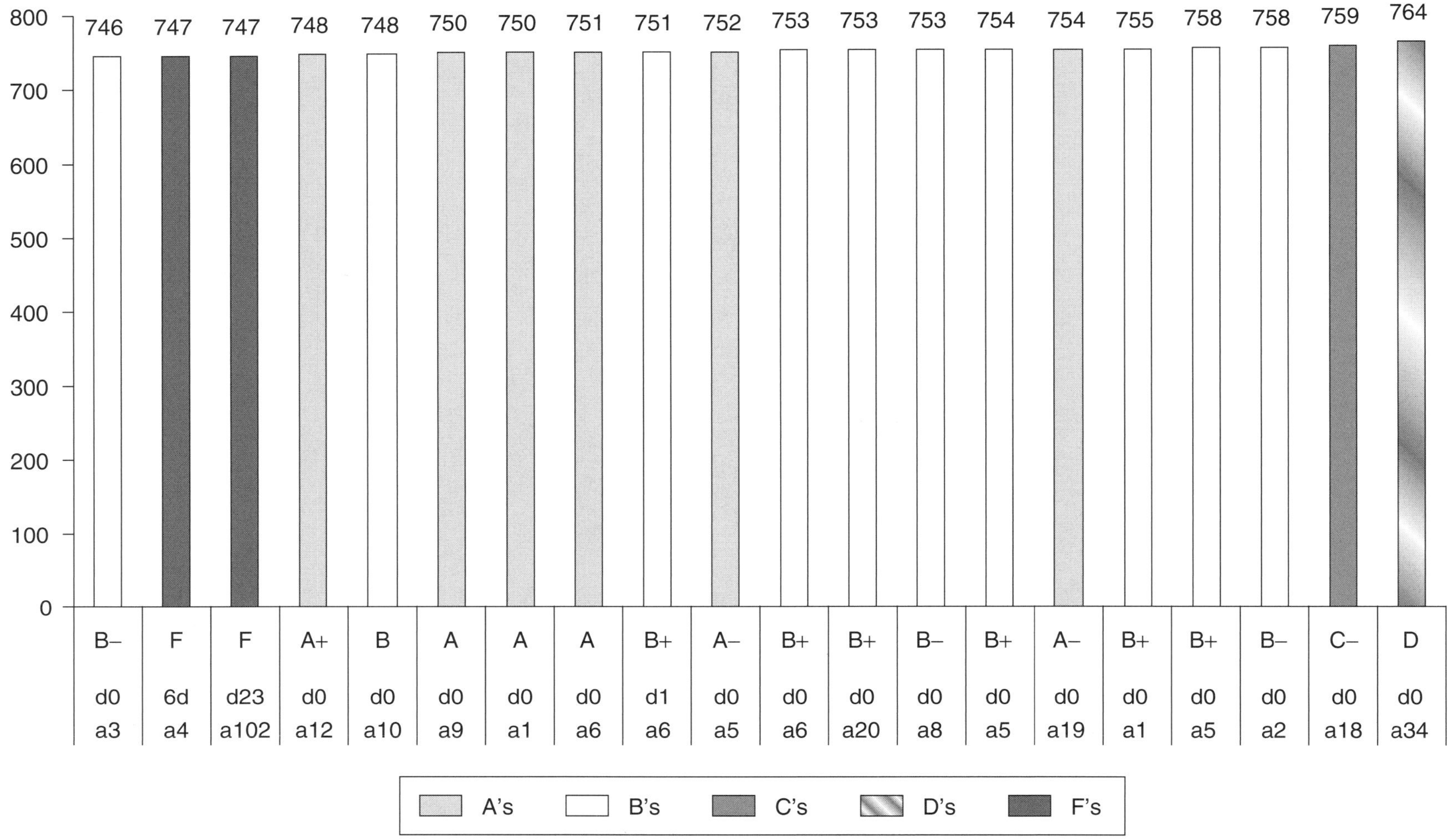

Scale Score	746	747	747	748	748	750	750	751	751	752	753	753	753	754	754	755	758	758	759	764
Grade	B−	F	F	A+	B	A	A	A	B+	A−	B+	B+	B−	B+	A−	B+	B+	B−	C−	D
Discipline	d0	6d	d23	d0	d0	d0	d0	d0	d1	d0	d0	d0	d0	d0	d0	d0	d0	d0	d0	d0
Absences	a3	a4	a102	a12	a10	a9	a1	a6	a6	a5	a6	a20	a8	a5	a19	a1	a5	a2	a18	a34

Legend: A's · B's · C's · D's · F's

49

Viewing all twenty pages of the graph gives a more comprehensive look at the data, but questions can arise from viewing only Figure 4.14. Some of the top-performing students on standardized tests are getting poor grades. Why? Some students with high absences have low grades. Is their lack of achievement because they are not in school, or are they not in school because they don't feel they can succeed? What other questions arise? What might these data indicate as far as an action plan?

CLOSING THOUGHTS

With the results of standardized tests come volumes of data. It is a worthwhile use of time to sort through the information and identify data most closely related to district needs, goals, and plans. To aid in the evaluation and interpretation of data, visual representations can be created. To help data team members with their tasks, choose a graph that represents the data in an easy-to-read and understandable format.

View different levels of data, compare types of information, and review item analyses. Encourage questions. Follow through by providing data that may support answers. An answer may not surface, but more discussion will follow. Discussions often lead to the need for more data, followed by more discussions, followed by more questions, followed by more data. Eventually though, you will gain valuable insights into aspects of your school and district. Using those insights, you can lay the groundwork for improvement processes and increased future success. You become data reliant. Your decisions are data based. That's a wonderful place to be.

5

Using District
Assessments

DISTRICT ASSESSMENTS

District and benchmark assessments are becoming increasing popular in efforts to improve student achievement. Progress-monitoring tests such as these provide feedback to students, teachers, and districts periodically throughout the year, as opposed to standardized tests, which measure annual progress. District assessments can provide checkpoints throughout the year to determine whether students are progressing as needed to meet state and district standards.

One of the most essential components of district-level assessments is their ability to establish learning targets for teachers and students. These assessments enable evaluation of key pieces of understanding. They clearly reveal the teaching and learning targets. When there is more than one classroom per grade level, or more than one school per district, the assessment clarifies the end goal. It answers the question, what do we want students to know, do, and apply? What is important? Districts can also be assured that students in schools across the district have the same focus. The district-level assessments provide evidence regarding the extent of students' knowledge and ability to apply learning. They give teachers additional data about classroom performance and comparisons between groups of students.

District assessments provide districts and schools with a level of data not available in standardized or classroom assessments. Student progress can be measured specifically on district standards and curriculum. Results comparisons can be made between schools and between classrooms. With standardized assessments, the standards being measured do not necessarily coincide with those of the districts. Classroom assessments are often

Figure 5.1   Complete Assessment Package Diagram

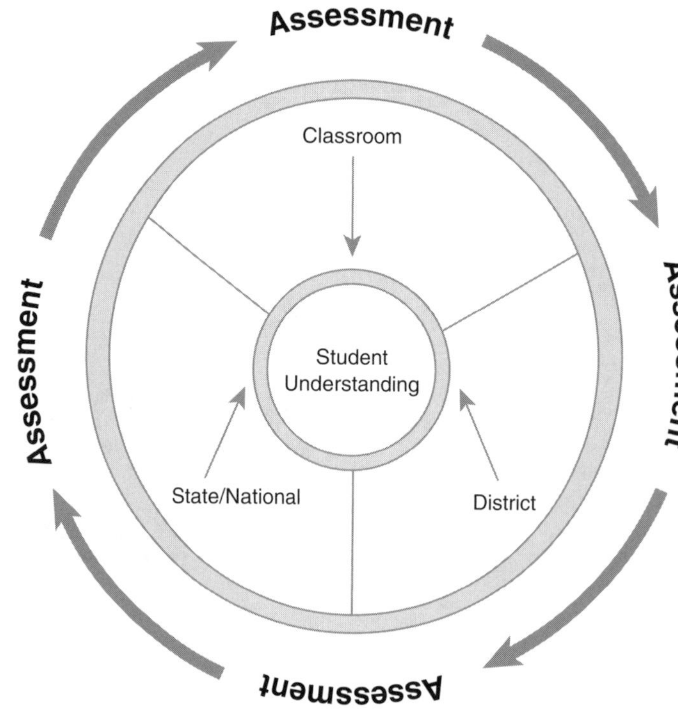

classroom specific and not comparable outside of the classroom. However, they provide valuable student-to-student and student-to-self comparisons.

Figure 5.1 illustrates a complete assessment package. Through the use of ongoing quality assessments and the analysis of student performance on those measures, educators gain a well-rounded look at student understanding. If any of the three main components are missing, the picture is not complete.

COLLECTING THE DATA

District assessment data need to be collected at the district level. This sounds fairly obvious, but this step can be easily missed, especially when district-level assessments are new to the process. Certainly, educators are accustomed to gathering classroom data when they are in the classroom. At the district level, educators receive standardized data. When using district assessments, educators are basically collecting classroom data at the district level.

To create a smooth collection process, timelines and expectations should be clear and up front. Consider answers to the questions shown in Figure 5.2.

WHY COLLECT AND SHARE?

The purposes of collecting and reporting district data are varied. One is to provide information to administrators, teachers, and students regarding

Figure 5.2   District Assessment Implementation and Data Collection Plan

Assessment Title: _____

On what date(s) will the assessment be administered?

Which students will be taking the assessment?

Who will score the assessments?

Who will record the results?

In what format will the results be collected (e.g., paper, spreadsheet)?

Who will collect and compile the results for the entire district?

By when are the results due?

How will results be reported? By district, school, or classroom?

In what format will the results be reported (e.g., charts, graphs, tables)?

How will the results be shared?

With whom will the results be shared?

How will the results be used to influence instruction?

Copyright © 2006 by Corwin Press. All rights reserved. Reprinted from *The Data Guidebook for Teachers and Leaders: Tools for Continuous Improvement,* by Eileen Depka. Thousand Oaks, CA: Corwin Press, www.corwinpress.com. Reproduction authorized only for the local school site or nonprofit organization that has purchased this book.

students' performance on assessments that evaluate district expectations. These assessment tools either are created by the district or are purchased because they directly align with the local curriculum. They test what is taught, and the evaluation of the learning is meaningful to all stakeholders. As a result, progress on these assessments is essential.

With district data, comparisons are not only possible but necessary. School, classroom, and student performance can be reviewed. Similarities, differences, strengths, and challenges surface. The results provide the perfect fuel for discussion and planning. Teachers need the opportunity to speculate about the results, share their effective strategies, and ask about the practices of others. These discussions are the catalyst for change. To influence student results, teachers use the expertise of their colleagues to expand their own bank of best practices.

The role of the administrator is important to the process as well. Communication between schools expands the bank of knowledge, experience, and strategies that are available within a single location. Soliciting the expertise of others across the district increases the effectiveness of all. Time and opportunity need to be provided for valuable discussions to occur. Principals should not only support the sharing and learning process of teachers, but they should also become actively involved in dialogue as well. Which proven practices from other schools can principals encourage and support in their own schools? How can principals expand their bank of knowledge and understanding to better support effective classroom practices? What are the needs of their teachers? How can their needs be addressed successfully?

CLOSING THOUGHTS

The use of district assessments provides valuable data to complete an achievement picture. The data provide comparisons between classrooms, grade levels, and schools, comparisons that are not available with classroom assessments. District-level tests supply results directly related to local curriculum, which is not always the case with standardized tests. Quality district, school, and classroom discussions, decisions, and plans are possible using results from district assessments because of the assessments' close relationship with district standards and curriculum. Standardized tests provide data for districts and schools. Classroom assessments provide information for the classroom teacher and the students. District results create a data source valuable to the district, its schools, its classrooms, and its students. The value is not only in the district's assessment of learning but also in its delivery of data, which can be used to make instructional decisions during the year, directing the instructional path of teachers and the learning route of students.

District assessment data should include the same views of data mentioned in previous chapters. Longitudinal data is needed, and disaggregated data is key.

6

Rubrics

Data Use and Organization

GAINING A COMMON UNDERSTANDING: HOLISTIC AND ANALYTICAL RUBRICS

The use of rubrics in education is widespread and beneficial. Rubrics help students gain a better understanding of quality and, as a result, potentially achieve a higher level of performance.

The word "rubric" is often used to describe a variety of scoring guides. To establish a common understanding, the following definition is used. A "rubric" is a scoring guide with specific, well-written indicators of quality at various levels of performance within a specific point scale.

When creating a rubric, educators should follow three basic steps:

1. Choose a point scale.

2. Identify criteria that will lead to the successful completion of the product, project, or performance to be evaluated.

3. Write descriptors of quality for each criterion at each point value.

Two commonly used rubrics are the holistic rubric and the analytical rubric. The holistic rubric has several descriptors for each point value. Students are assigned one number indicating the level of their performance. The analytical rubric is used differently. A descriptor is written for each criterion at each point value. Students are assigned a performance

Figure 6.1   Holistic Rubric

PowerPoint Presentation Rubric: Mrs. Smith's Fourth-Grade Class	
4 Points	• Title has accurate spelling and capitalization, relates to the project, and catches audience interest. • Eight slides include at least four related pictures and two related graphs or charts. Color, sound, and transitions enhance presentation. • Each slide contains accurate, easy-to-understand, in-depth information to support the topic.
3 Points	• Title has accurate spelling and capitalization and relates to the project. • Eight slides include at least four related pictures and two related graphs or charts. • Each slide contains accurate, easy-to-understand information to support the topic.
2 Points	• Title has accurate spelling and capitalization. • Eight slides include at least four related pictures. • Each slide contains accurate, easy-to-understand information to support the topic.
1 Point	• Title is present. • Eight slides are present. • Information in each slide supports the topic.

level for each criterion on which they are evaluated. Figure 6.1 shows an example of a holistic rubric. Figure 6.2 illustrates an analytical rubric.

Parallel construction is used when designing the holistic rubric. In other words, each line within each point value deals with the same criterion as its corresponding line in the next point value. In the holistic rubric in Figure 6.1, the first line relates to the title, the second to the slides, and the third to the information within each point value. When evaluated using this rubric, students receive a single score for their presentation.

When designing an analytical rubric, it is important to write descriptors in such a way that students cannot fall between point values. It is equally important that there is not so much information within a descriptor that students can fall within multiple point values at the same time. When using an analytical rubric, assign students a score for each of the criteria listed on the left side of the rubric. They might, for example, receive 2 points for title, 4 points for slides, and 3 points for information.

The construction and use of a good rubric leads to the beneficial use of data. Well-chosen criteria and clear, meaningful descriptors help students and teachers evaluate results and outline an improvement path.

GATHERING INDIVIDUAL STUDENT DATA FROM RUBRICS

Holistic rubrics provide some information to students, but it is not as defined as the information gleaned from analytical rubrics. When given

Figure 6.2   Analytical Rubric

PowerPoint Presentation Rubric: Mrs. Smith's Fourth-Grade Class				
Criterion	1 = Minimal	2 = Basic	3 = Proficient	4 = Advanced
Title	• Present	• Present • Accurate spelling and capitalization	• Present • Accurate spelling and capitalization • Relates to the project	• Present • Accurate spelling and capitalization • Relates to the project • Catches interest of audience
Slides	• Eight slides	• Eight slides • Four or more related pictures	• Eight slides • Four or more related pictures • Two or more related graphs/charts	• Eight slides • Four or more related pictures • Two or more related graphs/charts • Enhancing color, sound, and transitions
Information	• Information to support topic in each slide	• Accurate information to support topic in each slide	• Accurate, easy-to-understand information to support topic in each slide	• Accurate, easy-to-understand, in-depth information to support topic in each slide

one score with multiple descriptors, as is the case with holistic rubrics, it is possible for an entire product to fall outside a specific point value when some of the product may be more accurately placed elsewhere. Figure 6.3 provides an example of this situation.

For example, in the holistic rubric shown in Figure 6.3, a student may have used rich, elaborate descriptive words and earned 4 points but had no apparent conclusion, which is worth only 1 point. Because the student is given only one score, the score will not accurately reflect the performance. Teachers often highlight or check the descriptions that best fit the student's work. This is quite helpful. An alternative would be to use an analytical form of the same rubric, which would serve the same purpose and give students more detailed information about the assessment of their product.

When using an analytical rubric, teachers may choose to highlight the descriptor for each criterion that best describes the product, or they may simply place an "x" in the box. When the rubric is complete, there should be a mark within one box for each horizontal category. In other words, a point value is assigned to each criterion. A product evaluated with the rubric in Figure 6.4 would receive a score in each of thirteen areas, giving the students detailed information and a pathway for improvement.

Figure 6.3 Middle School Holistic Writing Rubric

Middle School Writing Rubric	
4 Points	• Rich, elaborate use of descriptive words that are audience appropriate • Varied and interesting sentences • No fragments, run-ons, or mechanical errors • Attention-grabbing introduction • Order that enhances understanding • Effective conclusion that ties pieces together and provides closure • Specific, well-developed, details that enhance and clarify the topic • Effective transitions within and between paragraphs, creating smooth flow • Thought-provoking, clear, focused, and insightful ideas • Lively, expressive, and engaging tone that captivates and keeps attention
3 Points	• Effective use of descriptive words • Varied, easy-to-understand sentences • A few fragments, run-ons, and errors that do not interfere with understanding • Interesting introduction • Understandable order • Conclusion that summarizes key points and restates main ideas • Effective use of details • Effective transitions • Clear and consistent ideas • Tone that expresses individual personality and interest in topic
2 Points	• Limited use of descriptive words • Limited sentence variety • Fragments, run-ons, and errors that interfere with understanding • Introduction that makes an unsuccessful attempt at capturing attention • Order that interferes with understanding • Confusing conclusion • Repetitive details or irrelevant details that do not relate to the topic • Few transitions or ineffective attempts to transition • Unclear ideas • Tone that shows some interest in topic or attempts individual expression
1 Point	• Simple, ordinary words • Sentences all have the same structure; no variety in sentence structure • Fragments, run-ons, and errors that prevent understanding • Introduction that makes no attempt at capturing attention • No understandable order of ideas • No apparent conclusion • Nonexistent or unrelated details • No transitions • No apparent main idea • No apparent focus • Lacks personality and interest in topic

Figure 6.4   Middle School Analytical Writing Rubric

Middle School Writing Rubric

Criterion		1 Point	2 Points	3 Points	4 Points
Words	Variety/Complexity	Simple, ordinary words	Limited use of descriptive words	Effective use of descriptive words	Rich, elaborate use of descriptive words throughout
	Audience Suitability	Too difficult or simple for audience	Appropriate	Appropriate, easy to interpret and understand	Appropriate, easy to interpret and understand, interesting
Sentences	Variety	No sentence variety	Limited sentence variety	Varied sentences	Varied, effective sentences
	Structure	Fragments and run-ons that prevent understanding	Fragments and run-ons that interfere with understanding	Minor fragments and run-ons that do not interfere with understanding	No fragments or run-ons
Mechanics	Spelling/Punctuation/Grammar	Errors that prevent understanding	Errors that interfere with understanding	Errors that do not interfere with understanding	No noticeable errors
Organization	Introduction	No attempt at capturing attention	Unsuccessful attempt at capturing attention	Captures attention	Uses originality to capture attention
	Body	No understandable order of ideas	Order that interferes with understanding	Understandable	Order that enhances understanding
	Conclusion	None present	Confusing conclusion	Summarizes key points and restates main ideas	Ties pieces together and provides closure
	Details	Nonexistent or unrelated	Repetitive or not related to the topic	Present and related	Specific, well-developed; enhance and clarify topic
	Transitions	None present	Few used or used ineffectively	Used effectively	Effective use within and between paragraphs, creating smooth flow
Ideas	Main Idea	No apparent main idea	Not clear	Clearly stated	Thought provoking
	Focus	No apparent focus	Clear but inconsistent	Clear and consistent	Clear, focused, insightful
Tone	Expressiveness	Lacks personality and interest in topic	Shows some interest in topic; attempts individual expression	Expresses individual personality and interest in topic	Lively, expressive, engaging; captivates and keeps attention

REPORTING RESULTS

A rubric in and of itself provides feedback to students. Returning a completed rubric to the student is certainly one way of reporting results. Alternate forms of reporting can furnish a view that has a greater impact on students' understanding of the results. A picture of student performance is often easier to interpret.

Reporting results on a chart similar to that in Figure 6.5 is a good start. A graph of the data is an excellent tool for giving students a visual representation of their performance. The graph in Figure 6.6 helps students see areas of strength and helps them identify their areas of weakness. Using the graph in conjunction with rubrics helps students also see a path toward improvement. The rubric descriptors give students a definition of quality they can follow to set improvement goals.

This method of reporting is highly effective when used with projects, products, or performances that are repeated throughout the year. The chart in Figures 6.7 and the graph in Figure 6.8 help teachers and students evaluate current performance and view growth over time.

Figure 6.5   Rubric Results Chart

Words	Variety/Complexity	3
	Audience Suitability	3
Sentences	Variety	4
	Structure	2
Mechanics	Spelling/Punctuation/Grammar	4
Organization	Introduction	1
	Body	3
	Conclusion	1
	Details	3
	Transitions	2
Ideas	Main Idea	3
	Focus	2
Tone	Expressiveness	3
	Average Score	**2.62**

Figure 6.6   Rubric Results Graph

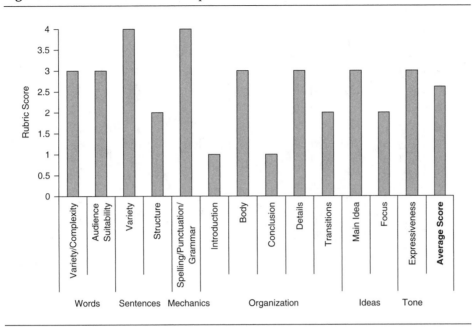

Figure 6.7   Rubric Results Growth Chart

Words	Variety/Complexity	3	3
	Audience suitability	3	4
Sentences	Variety	4	4
	Structure	2	3
Mechanics	Spelling/Punctuation/Grammar	4	4
Organization	Introduction	1	2
	Body	3	3
	Conclusion	1	2
	Details	3	3
	Transitions	2	3
Ideas	Main Idea	3	3
	Focus	2	3
Tone	Expressiveness	3	3
	Average Score	**2.62**	**3.08**

Figure 6.8   Rubric Results Growth Graph

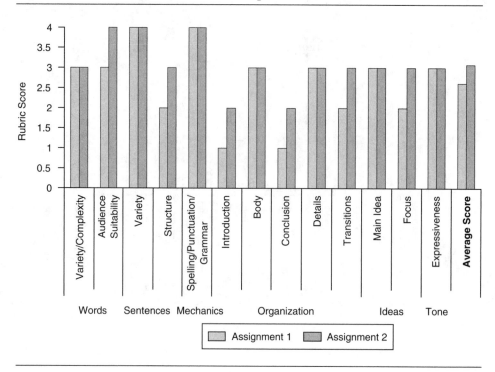

COMMUNICATING WITH STUDENTS

When sharing any results with students, it is important to take these three basic steps:

1. Distribute

2. Interpret

3. Plan

Distribute

This is an obvious step. After the completion and evaluation of an assignment, it typically is returned to the student. Often, this is where the sharing of results ends. Students see the grade, and the assignment is placed in a folder or in students' desks. The students may never think more deeply about their evaluation. To effect student achievement, the next two steps are crucial and should be expected of the teacher and automatic for students.

Interpret

Initially, students need help interpreting results. Providing time within the school day is essential for interpretation to be accomplished. After student rubrics are returned, teachers need to guide students so that they can gain an understanding of what they are seeing. For example, teachers might say, "Please look at the rubric results that were just returned to you. I'd like you to first look at the areas where your highest scores appear." Starting with the positive seems to work well. Some students don't see themselves as having strengths, but when using an analytical rubric, it is rare that a student would not have at least one score higher than others. We often forget to identify and celebrate successes. Teachers can then continue by asking students to pinpoint areas that present them with the biggest challenge. Next, students should locate the criteria on the rubric that represent their challenging areas.

Plan

Regardless of students' current scores, the rubric supplies descriptors for growth. Even students at the one-point level are on a path toward success. After students have located the descriptors of their current performance in challenging areas, they read the descriptors of the higher levels of quality. In doing so, the students learn what they need to accomplish to move to the next level of performance. After reading the descriptors, students plan action steps to move to the next performance level. A graphic organizer, as shown in Figure 6.9, can be used to help in this reflective process.

For younger students, the tool can be simplified. Figure 6.10 is an example of a simplified graphic organizer.

It certainly is not necessary to complete a graphic organizer with each assignment, but anytime students are given results, they should have time to identify their strengths and challenges, as well as reflect on what path they need to take to improve. Although the teacher needs to set the stage and provide the time for this to occur, the goal is for the process to become a habit for the student. The evaluation and improvement process can become internalized and automatic.

EVALUATING GROUP DATA FROM RUBRICS

Evaluating and planning from individual student data benefits not only students but also teachers, who make effective use of classroom or group results by viewing collective information. To create the graphs and charts used earlier to report individual student information, the results were typed into a database. That same file can be used to look at the strengths and challenges of the entire class (see Figure 6.11).

When a graph is created with collective results, a visual representation is formed that depicts the entire class performance on the project. This information can help teachers plan future lessons that address challenge areas, hence spending less time on the aspects of writing in which the children currently demonstrate proficiency. Collecting and organizing data can take time, but using the results saves time in the classroom. Data-guided instruction makes the best use of classroom minutes, resulting in student needs being more accurately addressed.

Figure 6.9   Reflection and Improvement Plans Worksheet

Reflection and Improvement Plans
What areas of strength have you identified?
What do you see as your biggest challenge areas?
What do you need to do to improve your challenge areas?
What help do you need from the teacher?

Copyright © 2006 by Corwin Press. All rights reserved. Reprinted from *The Data Guidebook for Teachers and Leaders: Tools for Continuous Improvement,* by Eileen Depka. Thousand Oaks, CA: Corwin Press, www.corwinpress.com. Reproduction authorized only for the local school site or nonprofit organization that has purchased this book.

Figure 6.10 Reflection and Improvement Plans Worksheet: Young Students

I'm happy about…	I want to get better at…	I will…	My teacher will help with…

Copyright © 2006 by Corwin Press. All rights reserved. Reprinted from *The Data Guidebook for Teachers and Leaders: Tools for Continuous Improvement,* by Eileen Depka. Thousand Oaks, CA: Corwin Press, www.corwinpress.com. Reproduction authorized only for the local school site or nonprofit organization that has purchased this book.

Figure 6.11 Writing Assessment Results Graph

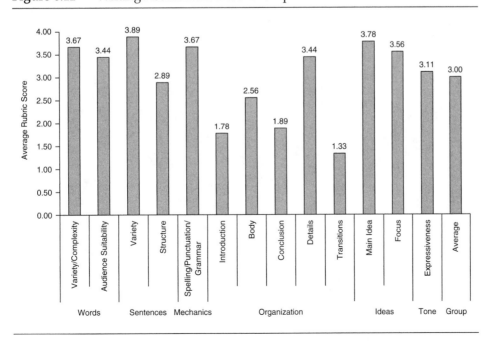

CLOSING THOUGHTS

Using rubrics with students benefits them by providing well-written descriptors that point students to a pathway for success. Collecting and organizing rubric data provides performance visuals that help students recognize their strengths and evaluate their challenges. Analyzing classroom results provides information that leads to informed instructional decisions and assists in making the most effective use of classroom time.

7

Classroom
Assessment Data

Teachers assess on a daily basis. In fact, they evaluate student progress minute by minute. Assessment, both formal and informal, presents teachers with sources of information to appraise student understanding. Observing student behavior, listening to conversations, reading expressions on students' faces, and responding to their questions all include informal assessment data. Formal information is collected from homework, quizzes, tests, performance tasks, products, and performances. Figure 7.1 illustrates a variety of assessment tools used in the classroom. A combination of these instruments creates a well-rounded picture of classroom performance. Data collection and evaluation are typically associated with formal assessment tools.

THE PURPOSE OF COLLECTION

Historically, one of the main reasons for collecting assessment data was to assign grades. The focus of education now places increased emphasis on student achievement. Education is not about how a student has performed, but how the student needs to perform to meet standards and experience long-term success. As a result, teachers need to use assessment tools to evaluate performance and plan for meeting the needs of groups and individuals.

Time is a precious commodity in the classroom. Teachers don't have an overabundance of planning time. Yet finding ways to make data collection and analysis manageable leads to data-based decisions and constructive use of class time.

Figure 7.1   Classroom Assessment Diagram

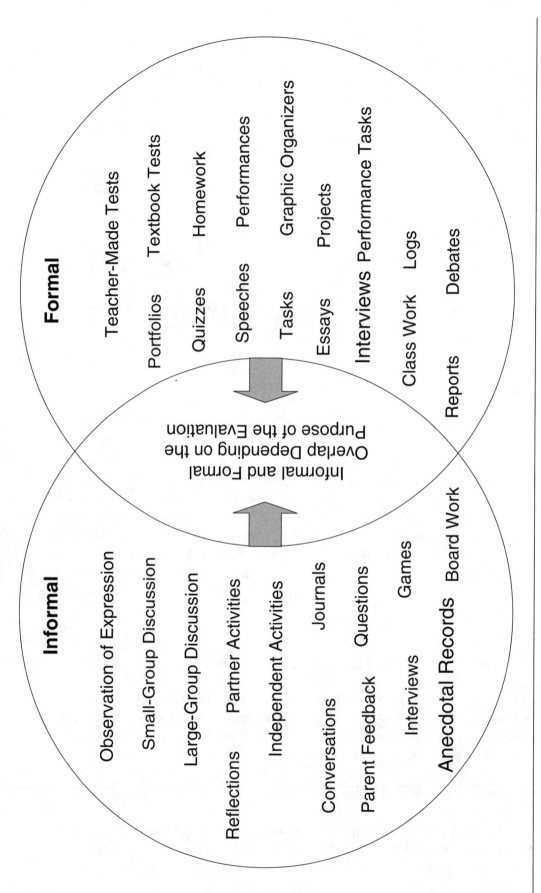

Classroom Assessment

Formal

Teacher-Made Tests   Textbook Tests

Portfolios   Quizzes   Homework

Speeches   Performances

Tasks   Graphic Organizers

Essays   Projects

Interviews Performance Tasks

Class Work   Logs

Reports   Debates

Informal

Observation of Expression

Small-Group Discussion

Large-Group Discussion

Reflections   Partner Activities

Independent Activities

Journals

Conversations

Parent Feedback   Questions

Games

Interviews

Anecdotal Records   Board Work

Informal and Formal Overlap Depending on the Purpose of the Evaluation

Figure 7.2   Grade Record Chart

Name	Page 108	Task 17	Quiz 1
Avers, Amie	78	90	98
Crants, Grant	25	46	65
Cravitz, Will	76	60	67
Deeka, Jonathan	100	90	88
Deka, Jessica	76	87	98
Garcia, Maria	87	95	88
Iris, Elliot	76	87	87
Jordan, Gordon	34	78	88
Matus, Monica	89	60	79
Smith, Dave	100	40	98
Welder, Grey	90	98	98
Winski, Barbara	87	87	87

GRADE BOOK HIGHLIGHTING

Highlighting is a simple but effective method for looking at data. After recording scores in a grade book, low scores can be located and highlighted. In this way, you can identify the students in need of additional support and the students in need of additional challenges. Highlighting creates a visual of those in need of occasional support and identifies students who are experiencing repeated difficulties. Figure 7.2 shows a highlighting example.

A three-color highlighting method can be informative as well. With this method, all scores are assigned a color, say, green, orange, or yellow. The teacher highlights in green the scores of students who have demonstrated that they are ready to proceed. The teacher highlights in yellow the scores of students who are achieving but not experiencing high levels of success. They may need additional time, support, or experience to gain a deeper understanding. The teacher highlights in orange the scores of students who didn't understand the concepts. This is a warning color: Without intervention of some type, these students will not have the foundation they need to be successful in the current unit of study. Teachers can use this color coding to plan future lessons and create flexible groupings. As work within a unit continues, success can also be clearly seen by the amount of green in the grade book.

ITEM ANALYSIS

Item analyses tend to be more time-consuming than grade book highlighting, but item analyses are a valuable tool when evaluating assessment results. An item analysis of an end-of-unit assessment provides a visual of how well the students learned the concepts taught. It also clearly pinpoints concepts that confused the students. Poor test questions can also be identified.

Figure 7.3 shows a simple item analysis. Student names are listed at the side of the spreadsheet. Across the top are the problem questions from the assessment. The assessments are viewed one at a time. A student's incorrect response is signified by an "x" placed on the chart under the question.

Percentage scores for all students in Figure 7.3 range from 80% to 100%. These results in and of themselves could be seen as quite good. However, through a closer look at the item analysis, you can see that there was difficulty with Question 17. More than half of the students answered incorrectly. Assuming that the question was valid, the results indicate that students were having difficulty with the concepts addressed. The implication is that additional teaching or clarification is necessary. Without an item analysis, this detail could easily have been overlooked.

CLASSROOM DISAGGREGATIONS

Subgroup results are as important in the classroom as they are in the school and the district. Within the classroom, however, subgroups are often too small to disaggregate. The same end can be accomplished by using the highlighting method for the identification of strong and struggling students. The results can then be viewed with an eye toward subpopulations.

Typically, disaggregations by gender are possible, and unelaborated periodic disaggregations can reveal comparisons of achievement. Figure 7.4 contains the same names and scores as Figure 7.2 but with the gender column added. In Figure 7.4, students are sorted by gender and averages are calculated on all scores. The results are shown. Questions that often arise as a result of these averages include the following: Is the difference in averages an important one? Do the boys, on average, typically struggle more than the girls in this class? Which boys are successful and why? What can be done to promote the success of these learners? Are other teachers experiencing the same phenomenon? Is additional information needed before conclusions can be drawn? The findings can indicate the necessity to incorporate additional strategies to best meet the needs of all learners.

RUBRIC RESULTS

Rubrics are an excellent source of detailed information about student progress. As an evaluation tool, they also clearly identify a path on which

Figure 7.3 Classroom Item Analysis

	1	2	3	4	5	6	7	8	9	10	11	12	13	14	15	16	17	18	19	20	21	22	23	24	25
Avers, Amie																	X								
Crants, Grant									X																
Cravitz, Will																							X		
Deeka, Jonathan																	X								
Deka, Jessica				X													X								
Garcia, Maria																				X					
Iris, Elliot					X												X							X	X
Jordan, Gordon																						X			
Matus, Monica																	X								
Smith, Dave											X														
Welder, Grey																	X								
Winski, Barbara																	X								

Figure 7.4   Classroom Disaggregation

Name	Gender	Page 108	Task 17	Quiz 1
Crants, Grant	B	25	46	65
Cravitz, Will	B	76	60	67
Deeka, Jonathan	B	100	90	88
Iris, Elliot	B	76	87	87
Jordan, Gordon	B	34	78	88
Smith, Dave	B	100	40	98
Welder, Grey	B	90	98	98
Avers, Amie	G	78	90	98
Deka, Jessica	G	76	87	98
Garcia, Maria	G	87	95	88
Matus, Monica	G	89	60	79
Winski, Barbara	G	87	87	87
Girls Average = 85.7				
Boys Average = 72.5				

to proceed for continued and increased success. Time allotted for students to evaluate rubric results is well spent. A detailed look at the use of rubrics is included in Chapter 6.

A SYSTEMATIC VIEW OF CLASSROOM ANALYSIS

The achievement cycle is unchanged, regardless of the level of data and the focus of the analysis. Whether delving for information at the district, school, or classroom levels, you can analyze, plan, implement, and assess. Although all assessment results are analyzed by the teacher at the onset of each unit, teachers should consider for which tests they will create an item analysis. They should also identify the types of disaggregations that need to be completed. Teachers can use the organization tool in Figure 7.5 to promote the successful use of the achievement cycle when evaluating results. Figure 7.6 is similar to Figure 7.5 but is intended for student use.

DAILY REFLECTION

Reflection, a highly effective form of analysis that may include no numerical data, is powerful. Spending a few minutes considering events of the

Figure 7.5   Improvement Cycle Planning Form: Teacher Version

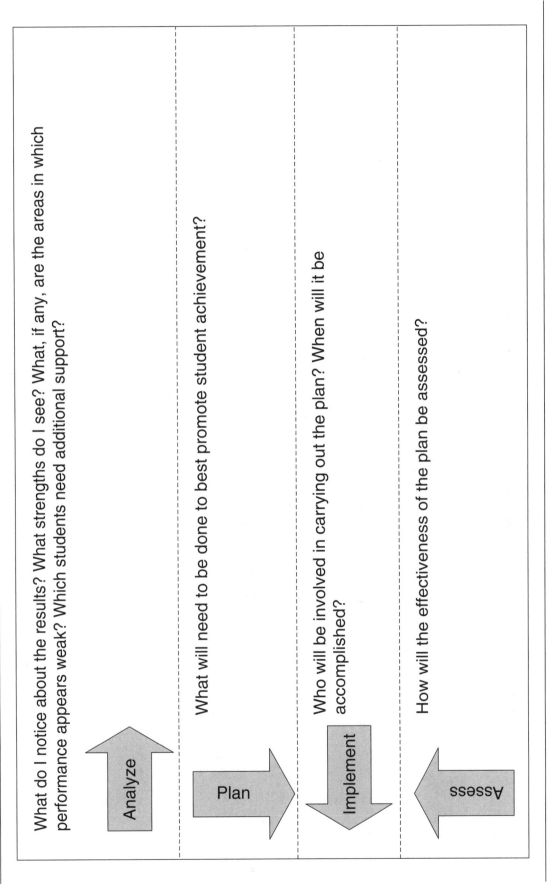

What do I notice about the results? What strengths do I see? What, if any, are the areas in which performance appears weak? Which students need additional support?

What will need to be done to best promote student achievement?

Who will be involved in carrying out the plan? When will it be accomplished?

How will the effectiveness of the plan be assessed?

Analyze

Plan

Implement

Assess

Copyright © 2006 by Corwin Press. All rights reserved. Reprinted from *The Data Guidebook for Teachers and Leaders: Tools for Continuous Improvement*, by Eileen Depka. Thousand Oaks, CA: Corwin Press, www.corwinpress.com. Reproduction authorized only for the local school site or nonprofit organization that has purchased this book.

Figure 7.6 Improvement Cycle Planning Form: Student Version

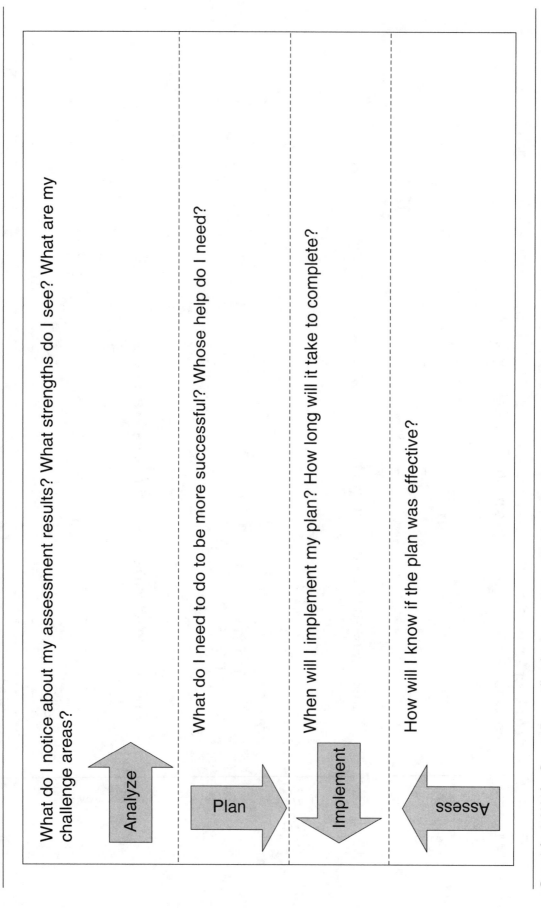

What do I notice about my assessment results? What strengths do I see? What are my challenge areas?

What do I need to do to be more successful? Whose help do I need?

When will I implement my plan? How long will it take to complete?

How will I know if the plan was effective?

Analyze

Plan

Implement

Assess

Copyright © 2006 by Corwin Press. All rights reserved. Reprinted from *The Data Guidebook for Teachers and Leaders: Tools for Continuous Improvement*, by Eileen Depka. Thousand Oaks, CA: Corwin Press, www.corwinpress.com. Reproduction authorized only for the local school site or nonprofit organization that has purchased this book.

day has an impact on instruction. As an example, consider the following questions: What went well today? What would I do differently? How will the results of today affect my plans for tomorrow? It seems that increased effectiveness and performance are the natural result when teachers give themselves the opportunity to reflect and then act on their reflections.

CLOSING THOUGHTS

The goal of an assessment is to provide students with a format in which they can demonstrate understanding and apply content. Using a variety of assessment tools furnishes students with the greatest opportunity to show what they know.

All assessments require a certain amount of analysis. It would be time-consuming to complete an item analysis for every subject or every class and every assessment. Teachers need to narrow the assessment field. Some tools are beneficial for a more detailed review. Through the analyses of standardized and district assessment results, you can identify areas of greatest need. You can also identify the assessments that cover the essential components of the coursework. Which formative and summative assessments are key in evaluating student progress? Which are cumulative? By selecting these tools, a more workable number of tests can be identified for extended analysis.

Data analysis is always part of the larger plan, which is to increase student understanding and improve academic achievement. For improved academic achievement to occur, teaching needs to be adjusted to best meet the needs of the students. This process requires ongoing professional development about practices that work. Teachers need to be given regular, consistent support to grow in their field. This can be accomplished in a variety of ways: Collegial study groups or professional learning communities might be promoted to support the acquisition of knowledge, book studies can be organized and promoted, a portion of faculty meetings can be used to share ideas that teachers have found successful, books and articles that highlight effective strategies can be shared, and professional libraries can be created and expanded so that resources are readily available and easy for teachers to access.

When classroom data are viewed, the purpose is to analyze achievement and promote learning. It is through the implementation of a variety of effective strategies that both can be accomplished.

8

Students and Data

As you consider students and data, the focus broadens. Data may include numerical results but also encompass student products and performances.

FEEDBACK

To grow as a learner, feedback is needed. Any information you can help the students discover—how they think, how they act, how they best acquire knowledge—helps them grow as learners. Providing timely feedback on products and performances benefits students as well. An additional, positive impact on learning and performance occurs when students are given the structure and opportunity to evaluate themselves.

Feedback can take the form of a comparison: the product to the requirements or the performance to the expectations. Nonjudgmental comments are effective in that the judgment is left to the student. The conversation that follows is the result of repeated opportunities to respond to feedback, in which the student becomes comfortable with the process:

Teacher: When beginning your speech on drums, the audience took notice immediately because of the way you began.

Student: I'm glad that happened. Instead of talking about the drums, I thought that by bringing one in and playing a portion of a piece I could grab their attention. It worked.

Teacher: During your speech, I noticed that you had five visuals to show the audience.

Student: Yes, I did. I knew that we needed four, but I thought all of mine fit with the speech and helped everyone to understand what I was talking about.

Teacher: When talking to the group you frequently seemed to rely on note cards.

Student: I know. I was nervous and used my notes more than I should have. Because of that I kept looking down instead of at the group. I think next time I'll write less on my note cards and use just key words.

Written feedback can produce effective results as well. Conversations are quite fruitful though and should be incorporated regularly as time permits. A two- to three-minute conversation encourages students to self-evaluate and ensures that they spend time thinking about their progress.

With younger students, conversations are equally rewarding. The rubric in Figure 8.1 shows the teacher's expected growth for young students when learning about numbers. The teacher uses the rubric as a discussion starter with the students. The teacher also helps the students become accustomed to using the rubric as a guide to continued growth.

Teacher: You were able to count to 5. That means you are at "1" on the rubric.

Student: What do I need to do to get to "2"?

Teacher: To get a "2," you will need to write the number "5."

Student: I need to practice it. I goof up and write a 2 instead. I know I can do it, though. I just need to concentrate.

Teacher: It sounds to me like you have a plan.

Figure 8.1   Number Recognition Rubric

Number Recognition	1	2	3	4
5	Student can . . .	Student can . . .	Student can . . .	Student can . . .
	• Count to 5	• Count to 5 • Write the number 5	• Count to 5 • Write the number 5 • Draw a picture of 5 things	• Count to 5 • Write the number 5 • Draw a picture of 5 things • Recite the numbers before and after 5

Avoiding words like "good," "excellent," "okay," "poor," and others commonly associated with performance, can be a challenge. But eliminating them from the evaluation can aid in the process of self-evaluation. Once students hear they have done a "good" job, they don't feel the need to evaluate any further. They are satisfied. If they hear they have performed "unsatisfactorily," they are not inspired to self-evaluate but feel more like complaining or making excuses. To keep an open dialog, state observations or factual information. This increases the likelihood of effective communication and self-evaluation.

Parents can also assist in this process. Encourage parents to ask their children about completed products. Questions that stimulate reflection work well: What were you asked to do? What do you feel you did well? If you were going to do the project again, what might you do differently?

REFLECTION

Daily reflection is easy to implement. It doesn't need to be time-consuming. It can be quick and effective.

We all need time to process information. During a school day, students may participate in as many as eight different classes with as many as eight different teachers. Younger students may have fewer teachers, but learning six subjects is not uncommon. How do they process it all? When do they have time to think about what they have learned? By the end of the school day, will they be able to remember what happened in the morning? When parents ask, "What did you learn in school today?" will the answer be "Nothing"? Students are exposed to a great deal of information in school, and they need the opportunity to analyze and reflect. In other words, they need time to process the new data their brains received during the day. At the same time, the teachers are able to collect information as to the effectiveness of their lessons.

Three minutes at the end of class is enough time for a reflective exercise. Several possibilities are discussed in the following sections.

Share-List Strategy

Quickly place students in groups of four. Students take turns sharing key points from class with their group. The rotation continues until ninety seconds pass. Students then have an additional ninety seconds to list the key points that were discussed.

Think-Speak-Write Strategy

Students spend one minute silently thinking of the key points they learned during the class period. The next minute is spent sharing ideas with a partner (thirty seconds each), The final minute is spent independently writing a one-sentence summary of the key points discussed.

Give-Me-Ten Strategy

Students quickly find a partner and for one minute share the key concepts learned in class. The teacher calls on ten volunteer groups to each share one idea with the class. Ideas should not be repeated.

Two-Four-Eight Strategy

Students form pairs and each share one key idea learned in class. The pair joins another pair to form a group of four. Each student shares a key idea with the rest of the group. Two foursomes join to form a group of eight. Each student shares a key concept with the others.

Stand Up–Sit Down Strategy

All students in the class stand up. The object of this reflection is to have as many students as possible sit down within a three-minute period. The teacher calls on volunteers as quickly as possible. The volunteers take turns sharing a key point from class. When the point is shared, the student sits down.

The Big Three Strategy

Students are given an index card on which they respond to three statements: "Name one thing you learned today," list one thing that you liked about class today," and "write one question that you have." When complete, the teacher collects the cards. The reflections help guide the teacher's plans for the next class.

Headline News Strategy

On an index card, students write a headline that summarizes the main point of class. Underneath the headline, they write a one-sentence summary of what they've learned. Students can also work with a partner in this activity.

Echo Strategy

The teacher says a key word that had significance in the lesson. Students echo the word and then write a sentence explaining what it means or why it is significant. If the activity is done verbally, volunteer students echo the word and state a sentence. The teacher continues choosing new words until time is up.

Have a Ball Strategy

Students form a large circle around the room and spend one minute in silent reflection, taking time to recall the key messages from class. The teacher tosses a ball to a student who then states one main point. The student tosses the ball to another student who states another key point. The process continues as quickly as possible until time runs out.

2L-1Q Strategy

This is a written reflection. Students are given a note card on which they write two things they learned during class. They also include one question that they have.

What Do I Think? Strategy

The student creates two columns on a piece of paper. In the first column, the students write the task that they did well. In the second column, they list anything they would do differently if they were to redo the task.

Written reflections can be collected and used as informal evaluation tools. Student comments and questions can help the teacher to plan adjustments necessary for the next class. The reflections can help evaluate the concepts that students understand as well as those requiring reinforcement.

CHARTS AND GRAPHS

Visuals can help students understand and interpret information about their performance. Chapter 6 includes examples of graphs and charts used in conjunction with rubrics. Students can evaluate and set goals according to the strengths and challenges illustrated in the data.

Standards-based reporting methods can also help students appraise their results by identifying the standard and level of performance. Figure 8.2 provides an example of the assessment results for one student on a decimal unit in math. Listed are the performance levels achieved by the student. Level 1 is considered a minimal performance, and Level 4 is advanced. The teacher provides three grades for each summative assessment, one for each of the following standards: computation, problem solving, and communication. Recording the grades in this manner gives more detailed information about student performance.

When viewing the information, students should be asked to evaluate what they see: What does the graph tell you about your assessment results? What do you think you need to do to improve? Class time needs to be devoted to this reflective exercise to guarantee that it occurs.

When Jon reviewed this information, he identified math computation as a strength. He felt confident in his ability to solve equations. Jon was aware that communication in math was an area of concern on individual assessments, but not until the results were analyzed collectively did he identify it as a consistent weakness. He realized that to improve he needed

Figure 8.2 Decimal Unit Results Graph and Chart

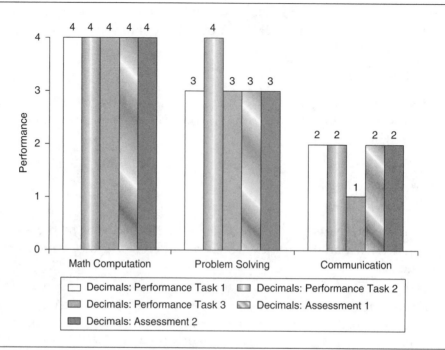

to make an effort to better communicate mathematically. After evaluating his results, he knew that he needed to take more time when explaining components of the tasks. At times this required asking for input from his teacher or parents before submitting assignments. He felt that, although he could improve somewhat by putting more time and thought into the communication process, he could also gain valuable feedback from others. Jon's thoughts and observations were recorded on a simple organizational tool like the one in Figure 8.3.

School-age children are not too young to view their own performance data. As with any new experience, they will initially need help, in this case with the interpretation of information. But they should be given the opportunity to self-evaluate and set goals using meaningful data. A long-term goal of student involvement in this activity is to help children begin a self-reflection and analysis process that may eventually become part of their own self-improvement routine.

CLOSING THOUGHTS

Student involvement in the data analysis process brings to mind the saying, "If you **give** a **man** a **fish**, he will be fed for a day; if you teach a **man** to **fish**, he will be fed for a lifetime." When students make a habit of analyzing their own performance, they can make a difference in their own level of achievement and performance.

Figure 8.3   Student Reflection

Name _____	Date _____
What do you notice about your performance on the data presented to you?	What needs to be done for your performance to improve?

Copyright © 2006 by Corwin Press. All rights reserved. Reprinted from *The Data Guidebook for Teachers and Leaders: Tools for Continuous Improvement,* by Eileen Depka. Thousand Oaks, CA: Corwin Press, www.corwinpress.com. Reproduction authorized only for the local school site or nonprofit organization that has purchased this book.

Three major components constitute student data analysis:

1. Feedback

2. Reflection

3. Goal setting

The greatest impact on achievement occurs when students are actively involved in all three components on a regular basis throughout their schooling.

Time is an important element when students are analyzing their performance. Class time devoted to this effort is essential.

9

Experiencing Success

GENERATE INTEREST

Data provide valuable information. Whether at the classroom, school, or district level, it is not difficult to generate interest in data. Data generate questions, the types that pique curiosity. Administrators need to expose teachers to the data and the ensuing questions. What can you do? Present data to those around you. Share your own observations and ask others to do the same. Ask questions and lead discussions. Create a climate in which data can be viewed and reviewed openly, without fear of embarrassment or retribution. What do the data show? Data show strengths and challenges. What can be done about what is seen? You can promote brainstorming. Regular use and exposure to data create a climate for and expectation of continuous data use. Data use is not an event but rather an ordinary occurrence in the decision-making process.

MAKE DATA A HABIT

Lay the foundation. Set the stage. The best way to promote interest in the use of data is to use data regularly and to expect others to do the same. Data need to become an integral part of the decision-making process. Before implementing change—a new program for example—ask what the data imply. Is this course of action suggested by your reviews and observations of the data? Districts are data rich. It would be worthwhile to become data dependent.

INVOLVE OTHERS

Students, teachers, principals, and district-level administrators should have access to relevant data. Collective opportunities to delve into the data might not occur unless scheduled. Gathering groups that can shed a different light on the data is beneficial to the review process. Different perspectives add insights. Involvement promotes ownership in the data, and ownership promotes a desire to find a catalyst for change. What can be done to improve results? How can we help students achieve new levels of success?

Identified weaknesses generate a sense of urgency. When challenge areas are recognized collectively, potential solutions are generated as a group effort: Educators are in it together; they are mutually supportive; they have a common focus.

Establishing and maintaining a comfort level is important to the successful use of data. Data often make people nervous. Creating a positive atmosphere of mutual trust allows data to be viewed and discussed openly. People are less likely to look for excuses and more likely to look for solutions.

If you're not careful, negative data can cause unfortunate reactions that are counterproductive to the atmosphere you work to create. The momentum you can build with the use of data and the implementation of improvement plans can be lost quickly if data are used to intimidate or punish. Remember, data is not bad; data just is. It's what you do about the data that is important. If you uncover a situation that you are unhappy with, openly discuss it and the brainstorming of solutions should follow.

PROMOTE THE CYCLE

An improvement cycle creates a process in which data are not only viewed but applied. The purpose of data analysis is to use the results to affect student achievement. Data analysis is the first step in the improvement cycle.

The next step is the creation of focused, meaningful data-based goals. Along with goals comes the plan of attack. What needs to be done to achieve the goals? What strategies will be implemented? What changes will need to be made? What professional development is necessary for changes to be beneficial? How long will it take to successfully implement the plan? How will success be assessed and measured?

Implementation of the improvement plan and the assessment of that plan follows. The implementation phase includes ongoing professional development and regular assessment. A laserlike focus is maintained. Continuous encouragement and support are helpful. Final assessments are completed, and then the process begins again.

CREATE AN EXPECTATION

For an improvement cycle to be an integral part of the district, an improvement plan must be developed at the district level and for each school in the district. Written plans are essential. Drafts are shared, adjusted, and finalized. The written document is a reference tool for the life of the plan. It becomes the document that guides school improvement. The plan creates a focus for all staff. As the plan is used, the process becomes part of the daily workings of the school and district.

All administrators should have the opportunity to view the plans of all schools. This creates an awareness of plans throughout the district. Schools can look to each other to share information and ideas and provide support. District-level administrators should be aware of how individual school plans coincide to support district goals.

Within a school, it is important for all teachers to see the district plan and review the school plan. Staff members can identify their individual roles in the improvement plan.

EXPECT CHANGE

If you take the time to look at data, create goals, develop plans, and then continue to do what you have always done, your results will likely get worse. Change is a part of the process. Expect that goal-focused initiatives will need to begin for growth to occur. New strategies will need to be implemented and supported by ongoing professional development.

PROVIDE SUPPORT

Resources are necessary to support continuous school improvement, and the support can take a variety of forms. Continuous improvement must be supported in word and action by the administration. To effectively support teachers, administrators need to be knowledgeable of best practices in teaching and assessment. Promote and support the beneficial practices that already exist within the learning setting and encourage their expanded use.

Proven, effective programs need to be supported. Evaluate the success of programs through the data they generate and the research of them. Eliminate the ineffective to make room for the effective. Give new programs and innovations the time and opportunity to take root and be successful and provide professional development opportunities in the programs.

Finances are also a key component of support. District budgets are limited. Money needs to be used to support programs and professional development that have the greatest impact on student achievement. This means that funding be used to promote new research-supported strategies that are most likely to positively affect student achievement. This does not necessarily mean that additional resources need to be allotted to the lowest performing areas. Doing the same thing with more money will not increase learning unless the strategies, methods, or programs were effective to begin with. If additional funding is necessary to expand or support the continued existence of effective programs, then increased allocations are essential.

The school improvement process is supported by increased learning experiences for educators and the promotion of continuous, sustained professional development. These experiences should be focused on student achievement and be directly connected to the district and school continuous improvement plan. Activities should maintain a focus: The object is not to see how many different activities teachers can engage in but how deep understanding of a few well-chosen strategies can benefit student achievement.

CELEBRATE SUCCESS

Through data delves, strengths surface and gains are identified. Spread the word and celebrate. It is hard work to institute change and affect student achievement. Educators need to acknowledge the work that they do to achieve positive results. Celebrations help maintain a positive atmosphere and advance the continued use of data. They also support the continued recognition and use of practices that are having a positive impact on student performance.

Another success worth recognizing is that associated with the school improvement planning process. Students setting goals to accelerate their own achievement is inspiring. Staff members working together to promote a clear, steady focus on student achievement is exciting. A district's members working together to achieve common targets is exhilarating.

Bibliography

Allen, P. (1996). *Educational issues series: Performance assessment.* Retrieved September 22, 2005, from http://www.weac.org/resource/may96/perform.htm

American Association of School Administrators. (2002). *Using data to improve schools.* Arlington, VA: KSA-Plus Communications.

Anderson, B., MacDonald, S., & Sinnemann, C. (2004). Can measurement of results help improve the performance of schools? *Phi Delta Kappan, 85*(10), 735–739.

Bell, L. (2003). Strategies that close the gap. *Educational Leadership, 60*(4), 32–34.

Bernhardt, V. (2005). Data tools for school improvement. *Educational Leadership, 62*(5), 66–69.

Black, P., Harrison, C., Lee, C., Marshall, B., & Wiliam, D. (2004). Working inside the black box. *Phi Delta Kappan, 86*(1), 9–21.

Black, P., & Wiliam, D. (1998). *Inside the black box: Raising standards through classroom assessment.* Retrieved September 22, 2005, from http://www.pdkintl.org/kappan/kbla9810.htm

Black, S. (1994, March). Doing the numbers. *The Executive Educator.*

Burke, K. (1999). *How to assess authentic learning.* Arlington Heights, IL: Skylight Training and Publishing.

Caudell, L. (1996, Fall). High stakes. *NW Education Magazine.*

Cawelti, G. (2004). *Handbook of research on improving student achievement.* Arlington, VA: Educational Research Service.

Chappuis, S., & Stiggins, R. (2002). Classroom assessment for learning. *Educational Leadership, 60*(1), 40–43.

Childs, R. (1989). *Constructing classroom achievement tests.* (ERIC Document Reproduction Service No. ED315426)

Costa, A., & Kallick, B. (1995). *Assessment in the learning organization.* Alexandria, VA: Association for Supervision and Curriculum Development.

Danna, S. (2004). Diving into data analysis. *Journal of Staff Development, 25*(3), 24–27.

Davison, M., Young, S., Davenport, E., Butterbaugh, D., & Davison, L. (2004). When do children fall behind? *Phi Delta Kappan, 85*(10), 752–761.

Dietel, R., Herman, J., & Knuth, R. (1991). *What does research say about assessment?* Naperville, IL: North Central Regional Educational Laboratory.

Dufour, R. (2003). Leading edge. *Journal of Staff Development, 25*(4), 77–78.

Eisner, E. (1999, May). *The uses and limits of performance assessment.* Retrieved September 22, 2005, from http://www.pdkintl.org/kappan/keis9905.htm

Gemberling, K., Smith, C., & Villani, J. (2004). *Leading change: The case for continuous improvement.* Alexandria, VA: National School Boards Association.

Geocaris, C., & Ross, M. (1999). A test worth taking. *Educational Leadership, 57*(1), 29–33.

Glaser, R. (1998). *Reinventing assessment and accountability to help all children learn: Introductory remarks.* Retrieved September 22, 2005, from http://www.cse.ucla.edu/CRESST/pages/glaserconf.htm

Greenwood Henke, K. (2005). *The data game.* Retrieved September 22, 2005, from http://www.scholastic.com/administrator/decjan0405/articles.asp?article=data_game

Hershberg, T., Simon, V., & Kruger, B. (2004, February). Measuring what matters. *American School Board Journal, 27–31.*

Jones, M., & Mulvenon, S. (2003). *Leaving no child behind.* Phoenix, AZ: All Star Publishing.

Kline, E., Kuklis, R., & Zmuda, A. (2004). *Transforming schools.* Alexandria, VA: Association for Supervision and Curriculum Development.

National Forum on Education Statistics. (2004). *Forum guide to building a culture of quality data.* Washington, DC: National Center for Education Statistics.

Northwest Regional Educationa Laboratory. (1995). *Research you can use to improve results.* Alexandria, VA: Association for Supervision and Curriculum Development.

Reeves, D. (2004). *Accountability for learning.* Alexandria, VA: Association for Supervision and Curriculum Development.

Repetti, D. (2004). The thrill of data discovery. *Journal of Staff Development, 25*(3), 28–31.

Rose, M. (1999). *Make room for rubrics.* Retrieved September 22, 2005, from http://teacher.scholastic.com/professional/assessment/roomforubrics.htm

Schmoker, M. (1996). *Results.* Alexandria, VA: Association for Supervision and Curriculum Development.

Schmoker, M. (2001). *The results fieldbook.* Alexandria, VA: Association for Supervision and Curriculum Development.

Schmoker, M. (2002). Up and away. *Journal of Staff Development, 23*(2), 10–13.

Sparks, D. (2003). Change agent. *Journal of Staff Development, 24*(1), 55–58.

Stiggins, R. (1995). *Sound performance assessments in the guidance context.* (ERIC Document Reproduction Service No. ED388889)

Tarant, L., Huebner, W., & Kaelin, M. (2004). *How do we know what students know?* Retrieved September 22, 2005, from http://www.enc.org/features/focus/archive/graphic/document.shtm?input=FOC-003560-index

United States Department of Education. (1993). *Help your child improve in test-taking.* Washington, DC: Author.

United States Department of Education. (1996). *Improving America's schools: A newsletter on issues in school reform.* Washington, DC: Author.

Wheaton Shorr, P. (2005, February). Numbers up: Six ways to make it easier to meet AYP. *Scholastic Administrator, 25–29.*

Wiggins, G. (1992). Creating tests worth taking. *Educational Leadership, 49*(8), 26–33.

Index

**CORWIN
PRESS**

The Corwin Press logo—a raven striding across an open book—represents the union of courage and learning. Corwin Press is committed to improving education for all learners by publishing books and other professional development resources for those serving the field of PreK–12 education. By providing practical, hands-on materials, Corwin Press continues to carry out the promise of its motto: **"Helping Educators Do Their Work Better."**